A Bible fit for the Restoration

THE EPIC STRUGGLE THAT BROUGHT US THE

King James Version

Other Books by Andrew Skinner

Temple Worship: Twenty Truths That Will Bless Your Life

Gethsemane

Golgotha

The Garden Tomb

Prophets, Priests, and Kings: Old Testament Figures Who Symbolize Christ

Verse By Verse: The Four Gospels
(with D. Kelly Ogden)

Verse By Verse: Acts to Revelation
(with D. Kelly Ogden)

Jerusalem: the Eternal City
(with David Galbraith and D. Kelly Ogden)

What DaVinci Didn't Know: An LDS Perspective
(with Richard Holzapfel and Thomas Wayment)

Scriptural Parables for the Latter Days
(with Jeffrey Marsh)

A Bible fit for the Restoration

The Epic Struggle That Brought Us the King James Version

Andrew C. Skinner

CFI | Springville, Utah

This is not an official publication of The Church of Jesus Christ of Latter-day Saints. The opinions and views expressed herein belong solely to the author and do not represent the opinions or views of Cedar Fort, Inc. Permission for the use of sources, graphics, and photos is also solely the responsibility of the author.

ISBN 13: 978-1-59955-908-7

Published by CFI, an imprint of Cedar Fort, Inc., 2373 W. 700 S., Springville, UT 84663
Distributed by Cedar Fort, Inc. www.cedarfort.com

LIBRARY OF CONGRESS CATALOGING-IN-PUBLICATION DATA

Skinner, Andrew C., 1951- author.
A Bible fit for the restoration / Andrew C. Skinner.
pages cm
Includes bibliographical references.
ISBN 978-1-59955-908-7
1. Bible. English--History. 2. Bible. English--Criticism and interpretation. 3. Church of Jesus Christ of Latter-day Saints--Doctrines. 4. Mormon Church--Doctrines. I. Title.
BS455.S54 2011
220.5'2--dc23

2011014416

Cover design by Angela Olsen
Cover design © 2011 by Lyle Mortimer
Edited and typeset by Megan E. Welton

Printed in the United States of America

10 9 8 7 6 5 4 3 2 1

Printed on acid-free paper

Dedication

For mentors and friends

Acknowledgments

No one is able to publish a book without help. Even a modest volume like this one is the product of many hands and heads. Three colleagues and I first embarked on an intellectual journey several years ago to understand how we got the King James Bible and its value to us. Thanks to a research grant from Religious Education at Brigham Young University, the four of us, Ray Huntington, Jeff Marsh, David Whitchurch, and I participated in a fast-paced tour of some western European countries and their libraries to fulfill our quest. We examined documents, took many notes and photographs, and shared in a rich learning experience. To them I owe much, especially for their friendship and insights. It was with them that I began to be profoundly touched by stories of sacrifice on the part of religious reformers and Bible translators—which led to this present volume.

I owe a debt to the helpful administrators of various libraries, not the least of which is the American Bible Society in New York City, for allowing photographs to be taken of actual Wycliffe, Tyndale, Luther, Geneva, and King James Bibles that appear herein. These libraries are the real treasure houses of humanity.

I acknowledge my ever helpful and supremely competent

secretary, Connie Brace, for her work and wisdom in assisting in the preparation of this volume. Those who know Connie also know of the great lengths to which she goes to make sure the work I try to produce is the best I am capable of. And she laughs at my stupid jokes.

I thank the staff at Cedar Fort, Inc., especially Jennifer Fielding, Heather Holm, Megan Welton, and the other behind-the-scenes professionals there, for giving me the opportunity to publish on a topic about which I have become passionate.

Last but not least, I thank Janet for her advice, kindness, love, and willingness to read what I've written, and especially for not complaining when I sequester myself in the study for hours at a time while the to-do list goes undone. She's the best!

Contents

Preface

It has been called "God's Bestseller."[1] It "has had a greater influence on the world for good than any other book ever published."[2] It served as the foundation for the restoration of the Gospel of Jesus Christ. It was a forerunner, preparing the way for the establishment of the dispensation of the fulness of times, of which it, itself, prophesied (Ephesians 1:10). And yet, no book has been more ill-treated, and few books, if any, have been the source of so many personal sacrifices to bring it forth! It is, of course, the English Bible. Elder Bruce R. McConkie said on one occasion, "Let me speak plainly. Satan hates and spurns the scriptures. The less scripture there is, and the more it is twisted and perverted, the greater is the rejoicing in the courts of hell. There has never been a book—not even the Book of Mormon—that has been so maligned and cursed and abused as the Bible."[3] And still, it has persevered.

Thus, it seems fair to say that the Bible not only records miracles, it is itself a miracle, including its development, transmission, printing, and preservation. To those of us who steer our spiritual ships by the compass of the English Bible, this collection of sixty-six books represents a divine library of God's revelations to, and interactions with, the human family.

(The word Bible, which derives from the Greek *biblia*, means "books.") But this great library did not come easily to us. Life was hard in former days. Still, God's will triumphed. Many of the events constituting the history of the English Bible and those whose lives are associated with it are truly inspiring. This present volume pays tribute to those who sacrificed for a cause they believed was greater than themselves—the preservation of God's word in a language the common man of the English-speaking world could understand. Many of these heroes gave everything they possessed—health, wealth, reputation, and even their very lives—for the single-minded purpose of making the Bible available in the English vernacular. Their stories are compelling. They are filled with high drama, self-sacrifice, intrigue, inspiration, intellectual brilliance, stupidity, scandal, duplicity, integrity, wonder, and awe. They are stories made for highborn and low. They are stories of persuasive interest to those who care deeply about their Christian faith and Latter-day Saint heritage, as well as to those who want to know who they are historically and how their culture fits into the grand sweep of Western Civilization. They are stories that define for us the meaning of the word *sacrifice* (from Latin, literally "to make sacred").

In medieval times, for example, scriptures found to be in possession of "unauthorized" individuals (those whom the Roman Catholic Church did not sanction, especially lay persons) were usually confiscated and sometimes burned along with their owners and readers. Not a few such individuals in the medieval Church became recognized martyrs. Remember, our English word *martyr* is a loan-word from Greek and literally means "witness." These valiant souls, who yearned to read and comprehend God's word in their own tongue and who were burned at the stake for their righteous desires, became witnesses for the truth by forfeiting their very lives. They exemplify the medieval Christian aphorism that the blood of martyrs became the seedbed of faith.

It is still shocking to many of us that such brutality was sanctioned by the medieval Church—the very body professing to uphold the teachings of Jesus of Nazareth, the One who promulgated such profound messages as the golden rule and love for one's enemies. And yet, it is a matter of the historical record that many copies of the scriptures were confiscated by Roman Church officials and burned with those who possessed or read them! In fact, there was a period of time when "[t]he first question ever asked by an Inquisitor of a 'heretic' was whether he knew any part of the Bible in his own tongue."[4] If so, that heretic was executed. Many of those truth-seekers were imprisoned, tortured, or burned at the stake—sometimes with their scriptures tied mockingly around their necks, precisely for their witness of the truth.

God himself will not forget these noble and great followers of the Lord, who suffered tribulation in their Redeemer's name. In 1834, the Prophet Joseph Smith received a copy of John Foxe's classic memorial work, *Book of Martyrs*, dedicated to those who sacrificed through the ages for the cause of maintaining Christianity in its pure form. After reading it, the Prophet said, "I have, by the aid of the Urim and Thummim, seen those martyrs. They were honest, devoted followers of Christ, according to the light they possessed. They will be saved."[5]

In October 1972, President Ezra Taft Benson elevated our understanding of how God views such men and women as those who sacrificed to bring to us the English Bible and who acted as forerunners in preparation for the Restoration of the gospel and the dispensation of the fulness of times. Then still an apostle, President Benson had just returned from representing the LDS Church at a celebration in Iran commemorating the twenty-five-hundredth anniversary of the founding of the Persian Empire, which served as the backdrop of his general conference remarks. He said:

> God, the Father of us all, uses the men of the earth, especially good men, to accomplish his purposes. It has been true in the past, it is true today, it will be true in the future. "Perhaps the Lord needs such men on the outside of His Church to help it along," said the late Orson F. Whitney of the Quorum of the Twelve. "They are among its auxiliaries, and can do more good for the cause where the Lord has placed them, than anywhere else. . . . Hence, some are drawn into the fold and receive a testimony of the truth; while others remain unconverted . . . the beauties and glories of the gospel being veiled temporarily from their view, for a wise purpose. The Lord will open their eyes in His own due time. God is using more than one people for the accomplishment of His great and marvelous work."[6]

This surely describes those martyred for their work to create the Bible in English in preparation for the Restoration as well as all who sacrificed for the cause of religious truth. Do we appreciate what they did? We owe them a great debt, for their sacrifices were not in vain nor inconsequential. No matter our place of national origin, ethnic background, or language skill, if we are part of the English-speaking world today, we have been influenced by developments in the history of the English Bible, up to and including the King James Version. In terms of sheer numbers, the English Bible has influenced more English-speaking people, religious and nonreligious, than any other single volume ever published. But more than that, the English Bible has been more influential on the Christian faith in modern times (from 1500 onward) than any other book produced.

In addition, a key element in laying the foundation for

the Restoration of the gospel of Jesus Christ in the latter days was the bringing forth of the English Bible, especially the King James Version. Religious reformers of the Renaissance and Reformation periods played a vital role. The Restoration owes much to the Protestant reformers. In addition to changing the theological landscape of Christendom, the reformers were instrumental in paving the way for the King James Bible and drawing attention to its doctrines and teachings, which were critical to the establishment of the Restoration. In turn, the coming forth of the English Bible aided the Reformation. The English Bible was "in a sense . . . a Protestant book"[7] and many of the Reformers sacrificed much for it as well as the greater cause they believed in. One modern prophet, President Thomas S. Monson, has described the Reformers, in the main, as "honest men with yearning hearts, [who] at the peril of their very lives, attempted to establish points of reference, that they might find the true way. . . . The reformers were pioneers, blazing wilderness trails in a desperate search for those lost points of reference which, they felt, when found would lead mankind back to the truth Jesus taught. . . . Significant was the declaration of [William] Tyndale to his critics: 'I will cause a boy that driveth the plough shall know more of the scripture than thou doest.'"[8]

Indeed, William Tyndale (1490–1536) is a superb example of one of the pivotal forerunners to the Restoration. His story figures prominently in the saga of the English Bible. Tyndale was an intellectual and spiritual giant, "one of history's greatest heroes,"[9] who suffered martyrdom to put a readable Bible in the hands of lay people. Truly, he exemplifies what is best about the Reformation's leaders and translators. One does not know but what his statement about the ploughboy knowing more of the scripture than recognized Churchmen of his day was a prophesy put into his mouth by God concerning the work of Joseph Smith, the prophet-ploughboy of the Restoration. Joseph's life and thought were rooted in the Bible. The Bible is the well-spring of the Restoration.

Though the Latter-day Saints are blessed to possess several volumes of scripture in their official canon, the Bible is not secondary to our core values. We are a Bible-loving, Bible-based people, firmly grounded in both the Old and New Testaments. In fact, our modern scriptures rest on the foundation-stone of the English Bible. We are a people profoundly grateful, or we should be profoundly grateful, for all those valiant souls who worked in any way to give us the biblical record in the English language. This present book attempts to explain why.

Like John Wycliffe, the first scholar to be credited with producing the whole Bible in English in the fourteenth century, the Latter-day Saints believe that the Bible stands as a yardstick by which to measure the morals, manners, and actions of God's children. The Bible is God's word, a rich gift and treasure to us, and if we seek to follow the example of our Prophet-founder, Joseph Smith, we will cherish it like he did. As he said concerning the Bible, "He that can mark the power of Omnipotence, inscribed upon the heavens, can also see God's own handwriting in the sacred volume: and he who reads it oftenest will like it best, and he who is acquainted with it, will know the hand wherever he can see it; and when once discovered, it will not only receive an acknowledgment, but an obedience to all its heavenly precepts."[10]

It is to this end that this present volume is written—that we might gain greater appreciation for our English Bible, but particularly for those who sacrificed so much to bring it to us. Though we cannot adequately repay our debt to them, we can at least think about them, offer prayers of gratitude for them, and strive to imitate them by living the principles they labored so hard to bring to those who came after them. This book is only one small attempt among many to vocalize our gratitude and keep the earliest heroes of the Restoration in our consciousness. As Elder Bruce R. McConkie testified, "The spirit of inspiration rested upon Wycliffe, Huss, Luther, Zwingli, Calvin, Knox, and others, causing them to rebel against the religious evils of the day and seek to make the Bible and other truths available to all who would receive such."[11]

The year 2011 stands as the four-hundredth anniversary of the publication of the King James Version of the Bible—a Bible fit for the Restoration. How appropriate that it also stand as a signal and marker for the time from which our renewed appreciation for the Bible, especially our English Bible, will have gone forth to all the world. Truly, the Latter-day Saints are a biblical people.

Notes

1. Brian Moynahan, *God's Bestseller* (New York: St. Martin's Press, 2002).
2. Joseph Fielding Smith, *Doctrines of Salvation*, ed. Bruce R. McConkie (Salt Lake City: Bookcraft, 1956), 3:184.
3. Bruce R. McConkie, "The Doctrinal Restoration." *The Joseph Smith Translation: The Restoration of Plain and Precious Things*, Nyman and Millet, eds. (Provo: Religious Studies Center—Brigham Young University, 1985), 12.
4. Benson Bobrick, *Wide as the Waters* (New York: Simon and Schuster, 2001), 11.
5. Edward Stevenson, *Reminiscences of Joseph, the*

Prophet, and the Coming Forth of the Book of Mormon (Salt Lake City, 1893), 6.

6. Ezra Taft Benson, "Civic Standards for the Faithful Saints." *Ensign*, July 1972, 59.
7. Benson Bobrick, *Wide as the Waters*, 16.
8. Thomas S. Monson, *Conference Report*, April 1997, 73–74.
9. Jon Nielsen and Royal Skousen, "How Much of the King James Bible is William Tyndale's?" *Reformation* 3 (1998), 74.
10. Joseph Smith, *Teachings of the Prophet Joseph Smith*, sel. Joseph Fielding Smith (Salt Lake City: Deseret Book, 1972), 56.
11. Bruce R. McConkie, *Mormon Doctrine* (Salt Lake City: Bookcraft, 1966), 717.

1.

John Wycliffe *and* Bible-based Reform

On a gray day in the year AD 1428, in the church of St. Mary's in the parish of Lutterworth in the English Midlands, an array of powerful men stood with a small crowd of local parishioners to witness the exhumation of the remains of the former priest of the parish. The bishop of Lincoln, Richard Fleming (in whose jurisdiction Lutterworth was situated), was there, along with the high sheriff of Leicestershire and his officers, as well as clergymen and lawyers, and a professional executioner. Yes, an executioner! The flagstones of the church floor were lifted, the coffin raised, and the decayed body removed. It was taken outside through a small door of the chancel—the same way the dying priest had been carried out by his parishioners forty-four years earlier after suffering a stroke in the middle of celebrating a mass in late December 1384. Once outside, the remains were borne in solemn procession through the streets of the town to a field near the River Swift.[1]

What happened next is both surprising and repulsive to modern churchgoers. A brief ceremony was held. Bishop Fleming proclaimed he was carrying out a sentence that had been passed on the former priest thirteen years earlier by the Roman Catholic Council of Constance, convened in

The River Swift, where Wycliffe's ashes were scattered.

AD 1415. At that time, the council had condemned several hundred propositions that had been put forward by the very man whose remains now lay in front of Bishop Fleming. The council had ordered that the remains of this vile heretic were to be removed from the consecrated ground of the Lutterworth church and completely destroyed. But because the deceased was deemed too wicked to be hanged, his remains were to be burned at the stake. Heresy in the fifteenth century was the worst of all possible crimes, regarded as so vile that it rendered even Sodom and Gomorrah pure by comparison. Thus, burning was the only recourse. The bishops that had met at the Council of Constance in 1415 proclaimed that the punishment due the dead priest was to follow him forever. He was damned "to absolute separation from God and to an eternity in hell."[2]

However, Church leaders were not allowed to carry out the sentence of burning, owing to the principle of *Ecclesia non novit sanguinem*, "the Church does not shed blood."[3] Therefore, after Bishop Fleming cursed the exhumed body, he turned it over to the high sheriff who, in turn, gave it to the executioner for burning. The executioner then chained the moldering remains to the stake and set fire to the kindling that was stacked around the decaying mess. After a time, he made certain that the bones and skull were so thoroughly burned that they had turned to ash, which he pounded with a mattock. The executioner then scraped everything into a wheelbarrow, sweeping clean the scorched earth so as to leave no remnant. The wheelbarrow was taken to the river and its contents dumped into the current. The instructions of the Pope had been fulfilled, namely "to rid the world of all physical trace of the heretic."[4] The name of this heretic was John Wycliffe, and the great crime for which his remains had been dug up forty-four years after his death and burned into oblivion was this—after calling into question the Church's authority and its errant doctrine, he translated, or at least oversaw the translation of the complete Bible into English for the first time in history.

We begin with this ending, of sorts, to focus our attention on the challenges associated with the coming forth of the first English Bible and to emphasize the courage, fortitude, and sacrifice of those who stood as forerunners of the Restoration. John Wycliffe faced violent opposition to his truth-telling efforts for most of the latter part of his life. But he was not the last to face calumny and hardship over his Reforming notions. For, in truth, though Wycliffe's earthly remains were obliterated, getting rid of his ideas was a whole different matter. The spread of his Bible-based theology by means of his followers, poor preachers dressed in modest russet cloth who met at impromptu gatherings in churchyards and marketplaces, was a major factor in revolutionizing the theological landscape of Western Civilization.

Education

Little is known of Wycliffe's early years. We first hear of him in 1356 as a junior fellow (graduate) of Merton College.[5] It is supposed that he was born about 1330, perhaps a little earlier, on a sheep farm in Yorkshire in the North of England. He probably received a rudimentary education from his parish priest. Around age sixteen, he left home to study at Oxford University, England's first and one of the world's most prestigious places of learning.[6] Here he eventually earned a reputation as England's most brilliant theologian of the time. In 1360, he became a master (professor) of Balliol College, and a year later he took his master of arts degree. Eight years after that (1369), when in his forties, he was awarded a Bachelor of Divinity degree. In 1372, he earned his doctorate in divinity. The many years of university learning speak to John Wycliffe's tenacity and unyielding spirit—attributes that proved both a blessing and a curse.

The social conditions that emerged during Wycliffe's lifetime contributed to an atmosphere of uncertainty and questioning. While he was at Oxford, the Black Death arrived in England. In all of Europe, between 1347 and 1352, about a fourth of the entire population died. The Hundred Years' War between England and France began in 1337, further straining relations between England and the Papacy. In England itself, an uneasy truce existed between the townspeople of Oxford and Cambridge and the university students (the so-called "town-gown" antagonism). The townspeople had become hostile to the invasion of robed academics ever since the founding of Oxford University in the late 1100s and the establishment of Cambridge University in the early 1200s. "The year before Wycliffe graduated, sixty-two students were killed by the townspeople [of Oxford] in a riot on St. Scholastica Day. For the next 468 years, on the same day, the townspeople placed sixty-two pennies on the altar at St. Mary's to atone for that misdeed."[7] These events profoundly affected Wycliffe and intensified his desire to find assurance and certainty in a tumultuous world.

Balliol College, Oxford University, where Wycliffe was Master.

Religious Imperatives

In 1361, the year he obtained his master's degree, Wycliffe was ordained to the ministry. After that, he undertook the Bachelor of Divinity course, which required intense study of the Bible in Latin. Therefore, it is no surprise to learn that Wycliffe fulfilled part of the requirements for his doctoral degree "by an unprecedented, if unoriginal, series of lectures commenting on the whole Bible."[8] By 1372, the Bible was thoroughly the foundation and centerpiece of Wycliffe's thought. At Oxford, Wycliffe became the preeminent theologian in the country. He was the leading speaker at theological debates, and his lecture rooms were always crowded to overflowing. The debates and class lectures honed his thinking and sharpened his convictions. His study of the biblical text led him to value the truth found in scripture far above tradition—even the tradition of the Church. "In Oxford, Wycliffe the fighter was born, and his sword was, above all, the Bible."[9]

Wycliffe's increasing concern over, and then combativeness toward, the Roman Catholic Church can be traced progressively in his writings. To be sure, he gave lectures to his students on the evils of the secularization of the Church. He loved preaching and teaching. But early on, he decided that the pen was mightier than the pulpit, the classroom, or the lecture hall. His earliest tract, written in 1360, was entitled *Objections to Friars*. It was not really an attack on the Roman Catholic Church but on the corrupt and ignorant orders of friars within the Church who didn't know the Bible or their theology.[10]

In 1376, Wycliffe published his first great treatise, *On Civil Dominion*, which was prompted by several years of watching the Church become involved in the world of European power politics. Some background might be helpful. In 1309, the papacy was moved from Rome to the

French town of Avignon and stayed there until 1377—a period known in history as the Babylonian Captivity of the Church (a parody on the Babylonian Captivity of Israel from 587–538 BC). This launched a further period of turmoil known as the Great Schism (1378–1417), when candidates from Avignon and Rome both claimed to be the authentic Pope. In 1409, the Council of Pisa tried to settle the dispute, but only ended up creating a third claimant. The Church didn't need three Popes! The Council of Constance finally resolved the conflict in 1417, but the intervening years were chaotic religiously. On top of this, England began their protracted war with France in 1337, which was actually a series of battles known as the Hundred Years' War. Thus, relations were already strained between England and the papacy when, in 1365, the papacy at Avignon demanded from the English crown the payment of the Peter's Pence. This was an ecclesiastical tax on the whole kingdom of England that amounted to two hundred British pounds per year, but which was then several years in arrears. The king and Parliament refused to pay.[11]

Wycliffe went beyond simple agreement with the decision of the English crown and publicly denied the theoretical and theological basis of the papal claim. Since Wycliffe was the leading Oxford scholar, people listened, and he gained a reputation as a strong nationalist. But his position also brought him into stark conflict with his own ecclesiastical leaders. In 1374, England appointed Wycliffe to a deputation sent to Bruges to meet with papal representatives regarding a number of disputed issues. But nothing came of this—except that from this time onward, Wycliffe's opposition to the papacy was adamant because Church representatives tried to bribe Wycliffe and others to modify their views.[12]

With this experience fresh on his mind, Wycliffe devoted

his energy and intellectual prowess for the next two years to an examination of the interplay of spiritual and temporal authority. Out of this came two other significant writings, *On Divine Dominion* and *On the Office of the King*.[13] His ideas have some relevance for our own day. His central concept was that the right to rule the people is found in grace, meaning that rulers, both secular and ecclesiastical, depend on grace (God's mercy and power) for their authority, and that "the clergy, if not in a state of grace, could lawfully be deprived of their endowments by the civil power."[14] Wycliffe believed that "if the high clergy (or the low, for that matter) are not living morally and therefore are not in grace, they have no right to their property and power. The function of the king is to sit in judgment on the morals of the clergy if their conduct calls for such action."[15]

Wycliffe was supported in his propositions by John of Gaunt, the ambitious younger son of ailing King Edward III, who also wanted the clergy reformed. He became Wycliffe's Protector. Reaction from the Church, on the other hand, was negative and unequivocal. The new bishop of London, William Courtenay, summoned Wycliffe to a hearing at St. Paul's Cathedral in London in February 1377. One reporter described Wycliffe's appearance as "a tall thin figure, covered with a long light gown of black colour, with a belt about his body; the head, adorned with a full, flowing beard, exhibiting features keen and sharply cut; the eye clear and penetrating; the lips firmly closed in token of resolution—the whole man wearing an aspect of lofty earnestness and replete with dignity and character."[16] Nothing substantive occurred at this meeting because a brawl broke out over the issue of whether or not Wycliffe should answer charges and questions sitting or standing![17] The session ended without Wycliffe uttering a word.[18]

More significantly, in May 1377, Pope Gregory XI

issued a series of papal bulls (decrees) against Wycliffe's teachings presented in *On Civil Dominion*, though nothing was directed at Wycliffe personally. However, in early May 1378, a number of bishops met at Lambeth Palace in London to consider Wycliffe's positions as outright heresy. No decision was issued, again owing to Wycliffe's support by John of Gaunt.

But, as noted earlier, in September 1378, the Great Schism broke out. Candidates from both Avignon and Rome claimed to be the rightful Pope. At first Wycliffe supported Urban VI of Rome but soon came to despise both claimants as the controversy proceeded. During this time, as he was researching and writing *On the Church*, which dealt with the roots of Church power and authority, he began to question the doctrine of transubstantiation, decreed by the Fourth Lateran Council in 1215, presided over by Pope Innocent III, the most powerful medieval Pope in history. In 1379 or 1380, Wycliffe concluded that transubstantiation, the act whereby the elements of the Eucharist—the bread and wine—physically became the body and blood of Christ, was not sound philosophically and was unbiblical.[19]

In 1381, Wycliffe published his views in a work entitled, *On the Eucharist*. Its teachings were immediately examined at Oxford by a commission appointed by the chancellor of the university and condemned. Even John of Gaunt withdrew his support and protection. Reforming Church political power and corrupt practices was one thing. Fiddling with sacred doctrine was quite another. Soon after this final blow, Wycliffe left Oxford completely and retired to his church in Lutterworth. He had become its rector, or priest, back in 1374 but could now spend all of his time there. He continued his preaching as well as his literary work. He maintained contact with former students and devoted his time to his most cherished project, the English

Lutterworth Parrish Church, where Wycliffe preached and was buried.

Bible, to which we shall return shortly.

Not allowing Wycliffe any rest, in May 1382, Bishop Courtenay, now Archbishop of Canterbury, convened a meeting of the clergy at Blackfriars Hall, Oxford, and oversaw the condemnation of Wycliffe's ideas. Present were bishops, many doctors of Divinity, a host of other clergymen—and Wycliffe. "They fastened particularly on the matter of transubstantiation. Did he affirm or deny this cardinal doctrine of the Church? It was out of character for Wycliffe to yield or modify his opinions, which had been shown him plainly from the Scriptures, and his response reflected this. He said, 'There was no fleshly presence of Christ in the sacrament, nor any other presence save a sacramental and spiritual one. . . .' He closed his defense with these words, 'With whom, think you, you are contending? With an old man on the brink of the grave? No, with truth. Truth which is stronger than you and will overcome you.'"[20] A few Oxford dons who tried to defend Wycliffe were quickly forced to abandon their support of him.

We must believe that the strain of the constant theological battles simply became too much for Wycliffe at this point, and he began to grow weaker physically. Then the inevitable happened.[21] The aging rector of Lutterworth was summoned to appear before the Supreme Pontiff. However, he never made the trip because he suffered his first stroke and was, as he put it, "hindered by God" from going. On the last Sunday of 1384, as he was ready to dispense the Lord's Supper, he suffered his third stroke. He died on December 31, 1384. Because he had not been excommunicated, he could be buried in consecrated ground.

But Wycliffe was not forgotten or left alone, even in death. As described at the beginning of the chapter, Pope Martin V had him exhumed and his bones roasted until there was nothing left. His own intrepid followers continued on, promoting the greatest and most cherished enterprises of their master—the Bible translated into English—to which we now turn.

Notes

1. This account follows closely the way the story is told, in even greater detail, in Brian Moynahan, *God's Bestseller* (New York: St. Martin's Press, 2002), ix.
2. Ibid, xi.
3. Ibid.
4. Ibid.
5. K. B. McFarlane, *Wycliffe and the Beginnings of English Nonconformity* (London: English Universities Press, 1966), 14.
6. Stephen H. Miller and Robert V. Huber, *The Bible: A History: The Making and Impact of the Bible* (Intercourse, PA: Good Books, 2004), 154.
7. W. Kenneth Connolly, *The Indestructible Book* (Grand Rapids, MI: Baker Books, 1996), 69.
8. F. L. Cross, ed., *The Oxford Dictionary of the Christian Church*, Third edition, E. A. Livingstone ed. (Oxford: Oxford University Press, 1997), 1769.
9. Connolly, *The Indestructible Book*, 70.
10. Ibid, 73.
11. S. Harrison Thomson, *Europe in Renaissance and Reformation* (New York: Harcourt, Brace and World, 1963), 173.
12. Ibid.
13. Ibid, 174.
14. F. L. Cross, ed., *The Oxford Dictionary of the Christian Church*, 1769.
15. Thomson, *Europe in Renaissance*, 174.
16. Quoted in Miller, *The Bible: A History*, 155.
17. John Foxe, *Foxe's Book of Martyrs*, ed. W. Grinton Berry (New Kensington, PA.: Whitaker House, 1981), 55–56.

18. David Fountain, *John Wycliffe—The Dawn of the Reformation* (Southampton: Mayflower Christian Books, n.d.), 28–29.
19. Thomson, *Europe in Renaissance*, 174–75.
20. Fountain, *Wycliffe—The Dawn of the Reformation*, 42.
21. Ibid, 69.

2.

The First English Bible

John Wycliffe desired intently to see the day when a complete English Bible was in the hands of everyone—lay persons, commoners, and scholars alike. He felt that the Bible should become the centerpiece of everyone's theology. The state of the Church itself caused him to see the hierarchy as corrupt and far-removed from the pattern established by the ancient apostles described in the New Testament. Thus, there was the need for a commonly understood "standard" against which the Church could be measured and that the English laity could read for themselves, rather than having to rely upon its transmission through the agents of a corrupted church. "The Pope was not the voice of God on earth, the Bible was," said Wycliffe. A revival of biblical Christianity was desperately needed; a reformation of the Church was required. The only way for that to happen was for the English people to possess the word of God in their own language. As Wycliffe said, "It helpeth Christian men to study the Gospel in that tongue in which they know best Christ's sentence."[1]

For Wycliffe, if an idea like transubstantiation was not in the Bible, it should be rejected. All teaching must be tested against the biblical text.[2] The Bible was the yardstick by which to measure the morals and actions of Church leadership as well as all men. It should be the center of Christian thought and practice. Scriptural infallibility replaced papal infallibility. "To Wycliffe, Scripture was a divine exemplar conceived in the mind of God before creation, and before the material Scriptures were written down."[3] Scripture ought to be the sole basis for Christian teachings. This is the genesis for the protestant concept of *sola scriptura*, "by scripture alone."

Before Wycliffe's era, only small sections of the Bible existed in English, or a form of the English like that which Wycliffe spoke. The only complete Bible available to most everyone was Jerome's Latin Vulgate.

St. Jerome (347–420), one of the Latin Fathers of the Roman Catholic Church, undertook his translation of the Vulgate precisely because of errors that existed in the versions of the Bible used in his day. In a letter to Pope Damasus in AD 383 seeking permission for his New Testament translation project, Jerome argued: "For if we are to pin our faith to the Latin texts, it is for our opponents to tell us which; for there are almost as many forms of texts as there are copies. If, on the other hand, we are to glean the truth from a comparison of many, why not go back to the original Greek and correct the mistakes introduced by inaccurate translators and the blundering alterations of confident but ignorant critics, and further all that has been inserted or changed by copyists more asleep than awake?"[4] We may compare this statement with one made by the Prophet Joseph Smith: "I believe the Bible as it read when it came from the pen of the original writers. Ignorant translators, careless transcribers, or designing and corrupt priests have committed many errors."[5]

Sadly, the laity were not allowed to read the Vulgate, even if they could. By a decree of the Church, the laity was forbidden "to possess any of the books of the Old and New Testaments, except perhaps the Psalter . . . but having any of those books translated into the vulgar tongue we [the Church] strictly forbid."[6] How different things are today. Latter-day Saints have more scripture than other people in the history of the world! However, if we do not read the scriptures (for whatever reason), the net result is the same as if the scriptures were forbidden to us because we are somehow second-class citizens of God's kingdom. In fact, if we do not read scripture, we make ourselves second-class citizens.

Wycliffe's attitude toward the Church's decree was, as toward other monstrous conceptions of Church leadership, contempt. He worked to overturn it by taking his case to the people. Wycliffe began speaking of creating a new Bible in English, just as St. Jerome had spoken of making a new translation of the Bible in Latin. Wycliffe also spoke of commissioning groups of his followers to go out as traveling ministers, in pairs, to present the teachings of the Bible to people in towns throughout the English countryside. One chronicler later reported with some sarcasm that so thoroughly were Wycliffe's followers disseminating the word that "every second man you met was a Lollard."[7] Later on, these "poor preachers" would disseminate English Bibles to those craving the word of God—literally carrying tracts and scriptures with them (sounds like Mormon missionaries!).

Church leaders bitterly opposed not just the notion of an English Bible but especially the idea of common people having the word of God in their own hands. Henry Knighton, a Catholic writer of the time and a constant opponent of Wycliffe, summed up the Church's view in telling fashion and provided an interesting window into the status of the laity in the minds of the Church hierarchy.

> Christ gave his Gospel to the clergy and learned of the Church that they might give it to the laity and more infirm persons. . . . But this Master John Wyclif translated the Gospel from the Latin into the

> Anglican language not the angelican. And Wyclif, by thus translating the Bible made it the property of the masses and common to all and more open to the laity and even to women who were able to read. . . . And so the Gospel pearl is thrown before swine and trodden underfoot, . . . and this precious gem of the clergy has been turned into the sport of laity, so that what used to be the highest gift of the clergy and learned members of the Church has become common to the laity.[8]

Wycliffe remained undeterred in his pursuits, as his response exemplifies:

> Christ and his Apostles taught the people in the language best known to them. It is certain that the truth of the Christian faith becomes more evident the more the faith itself is known. Therefore, the doctrine should not only be in Latin but in the common tongue and as the faith of the Church is contained in the Scriptures, the more these are known in a true sense the better. The laity ought to understand the faith, and as the doctrines of our faith are in the Scriptures, believers should have the Scriptures in a language familiar to the people, and to this end indeed did the Holy Spirit endue them with the knowledge of all tongues. If it is heresy to read the Bible, then the Holy Ghost himself is condemned who gave in tongues to the Apostles of Christ to speak the Word of God in all languages that were ordained of God under heaven. If Christ was so merciful as to send the Holy Ghost to the heathen men to make them partakers of his blessed word, why should it be taken from us in this land that be Christian men?[9]

Wycliffe's program was simple. Let all who could, read the scriptures and rely on the Holy Ghost for inspiration and interpretation. Wycliffe went to work in the late 1370s and persuaded scholars close to him to help create the new translation.

This new translation's date of completion has been the source of debate. Most likely, the New Testament was published in 1380 and the Old Testament added in 1382.[10] The new Bible was a translation from the Latin text of the Vulgate and not from the original languages, as William Tyndale's would be years later. However, it must be remembered that the Hebrew and Greek manuscripts allowing such a translation were not available to Wycliffe. In addition, classical Hebrew and Greek were little known languages in medieval England—or anywhere else at the time, for that matter. Therefore, Wycliffe's work was a translation of a translation. Regardless, Wycliffe and his associates were the first to translate the entire Bible into English.

Illustrated Wycliffe Bible

There is disagreement among scholars as to how much Wycliffe was involved in the translation.[11] But Wycliffe himself made reference to the personal sacrifices required of him in order to translate: "See [pointing to a table], it is there I sit not only by day, but often far into the night. Just a few lines will sometimes cost me hours and days of study before I can satisfy myself as to the correct rendering. . . . If God spare my life another year, I hope to put the entire Bible in English into the hands of the copyists."[12] This last statement sounds a lot like the one William Tyndale uttered a century and a half later: "If God spare my life . . ." And that is the point of all of this. God did spare their lives long enough to bless the world. According to a surviving copy of the first edition of the Wycliffe Bible, most of the Old Testament was translated by Nicholas of Hereford, one of Wycliffe's disciples and fellow workers. Thanks be to God for all of them.

John Wycliffe sacrificed everything in order to give to all English-speaking people the word of God in their own tongue. The preface to the Bible that bears his name contains a brief prayer that evokes the spirit and circumstances under which Wycliffe and his associates themselves toiled so diligently: "God grant to us all, grace to know well and keep well the holy writ, and suffer joyfully some pain for it at the last.[13]

To Wycliffe's followers goes our profound admiration for bearing the lion's share of work to bring the English translation to the public. His followers were immediately denounced by the Church and given the derogatory nickname of Lollards (apparently from the Dutch *lollaerd*, meaning "mumbler" or "speaker of nonsense"). The Church invoked the help of the state in suppressing and eradicating Lollardy. In 1401, Parliament passed a statute, "On the Burning of a Heretic," aimed specifically at Lollards. The

Lollard movement was driven underground, and many felt the flames of martyrdom, but the movement was never entirely extinguished during the several decades that followed Wycliffe's death. Wycliffe's ideas had tremendous staying power.

Impact and Legacy

In the England of Wycliffe's day, three main dialects were to be found. Wycliffe and his followers chose to use the Midland or Middle English dialect for their translation, which was popular in and around London. Unwittingly, Wycliffe performed a valuable service by helping to unite and standardize the English language. One gets a flavor for the language of Wycliffe's Bible by comparing a couple of its passages with their counterparts from the King James Version.

> Forsothe God so louede the world, that he gaf his oon bigetun sone, that ech man that bileueth in to him perische not, but haue euerlastynge lyf.
>
> For God so loved the world, that he gave his only begotten Son, that whosoever believeth in him should not perish, but have everlasting life (John 3:16).
>
> If I speke with tungis of men and aungels, sothli I haue not charite, I am maad as bras sownnynge, or a symbal tynkynge.
>
> Though I speak with the tongues of men and of angels, and have not charity, I am become as sounding brass, or a tinkling cymbal (1 Corinthians 13:1).

Wycliffe called people back to a biblically based Christianity, but not without great cost. Church leadership condemned the Wycliffe Bible, its creators, and its readers.

In addition to burning some of Wycliffe's disciples at the stake, a synod, convened in 1409 with the support of archbishop Arundel of Canterbury, issued a decree forbidding the reading of the Wycliffe Bible. Part of it reads:

> It is a dangerous thing, . . . to translate the text of the holy Scripture out of one tongue into another; for in the translation the same sense is not always easily kept, . . . we therefore decree and ordain that no man hereafter by his own authority . . . translate any text of the Scripture into English or any other tongue, by way of a book, pamphlet, or treatise; and that no man read any such book, pamphlet, or treatise, now lately composed in the time of John Wycliffe or since, or hereafter to be set forth in part or in whole, publicly or privately, upon pain of greater excommunication.[14]

People caught with Wycliffe Bibles in their possession were liable not only to excommunication but also to the forfeiture of all their possessions—their lands, cattle, and goods—and even their very lives. And yet, the threat of this kind of punishment actually increased people's curiosity and desire to read God's word in their own tongue, even at great cost.

Each copy of Wycliffe's translation had to be produced by hand, since his translation appeared almost a century before Johannes Gutenberg invented moveable type and produced the first copies of his 42-line Bible. Copies of Wycliffe's Bible were expensive, costing between £40 and £50, and took about ten months to complete. Forty pounds was the equivalent of about 9600 pence. A chicken could be purchased for two pence, a whole hog for four. The fact that Wycliffe Bibles are not especially rare even now, that something like 250 handwritten copies of Wycliffe's Bible have survived (far more than any other text in Middle English), is testimony enough that the book enjoyed extensive circulation in its day and that its owners placed great value on it.

Since not many people could afford to buy copies of the new translation, Wycliffe's followers traveled the countryside with biblical manuscripts for people to borrow. Sometimes people would rent the scriptures for a day or even part of a day. Apparently, the going rate to rent a Bible for an hour was a load of hay. To those who could not read, Lollard preachers read and explained the sacred text. Wycliffe's Bible, then, not only gave to England God's word in the vernacular, but it also increased literacy in the late Middle Ages.

One historian reports an interesting twist on the influence of Wycliffe's Bible. "[I]t is held by some, that when the citizens of London welcomed the first Elizabeth as their queen in 1558 and presented her with 'The Word of Truth,' the volume which she so gratefully received was a copy of the Wycliffite Gospels. We cannot be sure of this, but that would indeed have been a fitting climax to the history of the first English Bible."[15]

Though it may have represented a climax of sorts, such a happening, if factual, did not represent the end of the history of the first English Bible and certainly not the end of Wycliffe's influence. That influence continued to extend far and wide as asserted by one author: "Quoting John Wycliffe's Prologue to the English Bible (1384), [*sic*] Lincoln in his Gettysburg Address (Nov. 19, 1863) asserted 'that this nation, under God, shall have a new birth of freedom; and that government of the people, by the people, for the people, shall not perish from the earth.' "[16] It seems that the assessment of British historian Thomas Fuller was right. "They burnt [Wycliffe's] bones to ashes and cast them into the Swift, a neighboring brook running hard by. Thus the brook hath conveyed his ashes into Avon; Avon into Severn; Severn into the narrow seas; and they into the main ocean. And thus the ashes of Wycliffe are the emblem of his doctrine which now is dispersed the world over."[17]

Conclusion

Truly, Wycliffe's influence and energizing work had significant impact outside England. His ideas exercised considerable influence on Czech scholars, especially John Huss, who created "a short-lived revolutionary, religious republic."[18] After his condemnation as a heretic by the Council of Constance in 1415 (the same that finally condemned Wycliffe), Huss went to the stake (to be burned alive), having written "Wyclif, Wyclif, you will unsettle many a man's mind."[19] In Bohemia, Wycliffe was revered as no less than a "fifth Evangelist."[20] Through John Huss, Wycliffe even influenced Martin Luther, almost exactly a century after Huss's death.

John Wycliffe's thinking and his Bible not only laid the foundation for a great many Reformers, but it was the precursor of William Tyndale's Bible and, beyond that, of the Restoration of the gospel of Jesus Christ in the latter days. Truly, the inspiration that rested upon Wycliffe and those he influenced—Huss, Luther, Zwingli, Calvin, Knox, and others—"caus[ed] them to rebel against the religious evils of the day and seek to make the Bible and other truth available to all who would receive such."[21] John Wycliffe was the most significant of the early forerunners to usher in the Great European Reformation of the sixteenth century. One hundred and fifty years after Wycliffe's death, John Foxe (1516–1587), the great martyrologist of Magdalen College, Oxford, would write his *Book of Martyrs* (1563) and proclaim of John Wycliffe, "at what time [that] all the world was in most desperate and vile estate, and the lamentable ignorance and darkness of God's truth had overshadowed the whole earth, this man stepped forth like a valiant champion . . . 'Even as the morning-star being in the midst of a cloud, and as the moon being full in her course, and as the bright beams of the sun; so doth he shine and glister in the temple and Church of God.'"[22]

In very deed, John Wycliffe was the morning star of the Reformation, and the first in a series of heroes of our faith who loved the truth of Christ's eternal gospel more than life itself and who wanted the English-speaking world to have God's words in their own tongue so that the mists of darkness could be dispelled from their lives—our lives!—on a daily basis.

Notes

1. Quoted in Paul D. Wegner, *The Journey from Texts to Translations* (Grand Rapids, MI: Baker Academic, 2000), 282.
2. W. Kenneth Connolly, *The Indestructible Book*, 73.
3. W. R. Cooper, ed., *The Wycliffe New Testament* (London: The British Library, 2002), v.
4. James Stevenson, ed. *Creeds, Councils and Controversies: Documents Illustrating the History of the Church AD 337–461* (London: SPCK, 1989), 183.
5. Joseph Smith, *Teachings of the Prophet Joseph Smith,* 327.
6. Fountain, *Wycliffe—The Dawn of the Reformation,* 44.
7. Quoted in Fountain, *Wycliffe—The Dawn of the Reformation*, 53.
8. Ibid, 45, as well as several other sources.
9. Ibid, 47.
10. Wegner, *Journey from Texts to Translations*, 282; Miller and Huber, *The Bible: A History*, 155.
11. See, for example, W. R. Cooper, ed., T*he Wycliffe New Testament*, v.

12. Quoted in Robert J. Matthew, "A Bible! A Bible!" *Ensign*, Jan. 1987, 24–25.
13. Geddes MacGregor, *A Literary History of the Bible* (New York: Abingdon Press, 1968), 80; English modernized.
14. Quoted in Paul Wegner, *The Journey from Texts to Translations*, 283.
15. F. F. Bruce, *History of the Bible in English: From the Earliest Versions*, 3rd. ed. (New York: Oxford University Press, 1978), 23.
16. Gabriel Sivan, *The Bible and Civilization* (Jerusalem: Keter Publishing House Jerusalem Ltd., 1973), 239.
17. Quoted in Miller and Huber, *The Bible: A History*, 155.
18. Richard Tames, *A Traveller's History of Oxford* (London: Interlink, 2002), 47.
19. Quoted in Tames, *Traveller's History*, 47.
20. Ibid.
21. McConkie, *Mormon Doctrine*, 717.
22. John Foxe, *Foxe's Book of Martyrs*, 50. Originally entitled *The Acts and Monuments of These Latter and Perilous Days*, it quickly became popular as *The Book of Martyrs*. Some editions of the book show the chapter on Wycliffe to be entitled, "John Wickliff, the Morning Star of the Reformation."

3.

PRINTING *and* *the* WORD OF GOD

What John Wycliffe had begun in the last quarter of the fourteenth century did not—could not—die out as the leadership of the Roman Catholic Church had hoped. Wycliffe's basic points of reform found support far beyond England and gave laity as well as clergy a taste of religious revolution. His ideas affected almost all early Protestant Reformers in one way or another. In the words of one scholar, Wycliffe was "warmed with an eager spirit of religious controversy and desire for reform, [and] he developed those ideas and teachings that . . . carried his influence across intervening lands to a distant corner of Europe, [and] made his name famous in his own time and since."[1]

Many came to know that the source of Wycliffe's reforming zeal and fundamental divergence from the Church was the Bible. "Neither the tradition of the church nor the authority of Pope or council, he held, was of any weight in matters of religion when compared with the words of the Bible."[2]

Given the Bible's authority, Wycliffe's feeling that it should be made available to all persons soon spread to individuals in other countries. Translations of the Bible into vernacular tongues become an unstoppable phenomenon. The fourteenth and fifteenth centuries constituted "an age of translations, including translations of the Bible."[3]

In England, within two centuries of Wycliffe's death, "Scripture [would] appear in every home at a price lower than Wyclif [*sic*] could ever imagine."[4] On the European continent, parts of the Bible in French existed from the early part of the fourteenth century. But a new translation of the whole Bible from Latin into French was made between 1398 and 1407. Before 1300, biblical translations were available in Catalan and Castilian, but in 1422, a certain Don Luis Gonzales commissioned a learned Jew to make a new translation of the Old Testament into Castilian on the grounds that the old Spanish was outmoded and obscure. This new translation was completed in 1430. There were also Bohemian and German versions appearing.

Then, in the middle decade of the fifteenth century in Germany, Johann Gutenberg gave to Western civilization one of its greatest inventions—moveable-type printing. This sounded the death knell to pervasive medieval ignorance and inaugurated a spiritual and religious revolution. Within three decades of his invention, Gutenberg's achievement had been reproduced in most of Western Europe, and the world has never been the same.

Johann Gutenberg's Invention

The European invention of movable-type printing was, perhaps, the single most important development in the history of Western civilization from the time of Christ's resurrection up to the nineteenth century. It is not hard to see how God was behind this invention to further his purposes and to prepare the world for the Restoration of the gospel in the latter days. President Joseph Fielding Smith stated that in accordance with the prophesy of Joel 2:27–28,

> The Lord would pour out his blessings and his

Spirit upon all people and use them to accomplish his purposes. . . . If you will take time to reflect, you will find that in the matter of discovery and invention things have come about in a logical way, step by step, as the people were prepared to receive them, and each step has been in the direction of establishing the truth of the everlasting gospel upon the earth. Thus, when people began to study and to learn . . . and learning began to spread, the printing press came along and made it easy to publish books and other matters and to distribute them amongst the people, so that the entire people would learn. . . . There has never been a step taken from that day to this, in discovery or invention, where the Spirit of the Lord . . . was not the prevailing force, resting upon the individual, which caused him to make the discovery on the invention.[5]

The invention of movable-type printing was of such

Plaque from Mains Printing Museum showing Johann Gutenberg at work.

towering significance in the plan of God's work that the learned educator, Elder John A. Widtsoe of the Quorum of the Twelve, would state in a general conference address that our present civilization "really began when . . . the use of movable type in the printing press was invented." He then said:

> Latter-day Saints see even more in the coming of this great invention. To us it is part of the divine program to prepare the world for the Restoration of the gospel. Throughout the centuries, the Bible had been available only to a few. The cost of producing hand-made copies was too great for the common man to meet. The rank and file of the people learned of the hand-dealings of God with his chosen people from the lips of others, who often changed both words and meaning of the scriptural passage.
>
> The new art of printing soon made the Bible available to all. Learned men, lovers of the Lord, were inspired to render the holy scriptures into the languages of the common people. The Bible became a household possession. The word of God was read around the family fireside of the lowly as well as the parlors of the great. Humanity became widely acquainted with the eternal law of the Lord.
>
> Had it not been for the invention of printing with its gift of more perfect knowledge of the holy scriptures, and the equally new freedom of thought that followed, the coming of the gospel might have been long delayed. In that sense, we may date even the preparatory gospel period from the coming of modern printing.[6]

Johann Gutenberg was probably born in Mainz, Germany, sometime around 1398 or 1400. His birthdate is sometimes cited as June 24, 1400, because a leading Gutenberg scholar in the late nineteenth century supported Mainz's attempt to use the printer's name as a way to garner attention for the city and elevate its status. City officials wanted to celebrate the five-hundredth anniversary of Gutenberg's birth in 1900, and June 24 was already designated a feast day for John the Baptist, who shared Gutenberg's first name.[7] So, June 24, 1400, it was.

Gutenberg's full name was Johannes Gensfleisch zur Laden zum Gutenberg. Gutenberg's surname most likely derives from the location of property originally belonging to one of the many Jewish families of Mainz in the Middle Ages, situated in the area called "Juden-berg" (Jewish for "ward" or "borough"). In the late thirteenth century, many Jews fled Mainz following a period of anti-Semitism. This exodus included those who held the Judenberg estates. Gutenberg's father acquired some of the property and did not rename it, and thus it became part of the family's identification.

Gutenberg's education seems to have included attendance at the University of Erfurt, where he was exposed to philosophy and theology, as well as the religious ideas of Reformers like Jan Hus and John Wycliffe. By 1434, he had moved to Strasbourg, where he worked as a goldsmith and became adept at castings and handwork. In 1437, his name appears in Strasbourg court proceedings in connection with a broken promise of marriage to a woman from that city.[8] It was in Strasbourg around 1440 that Gutenberg perfected and unveiled to the world the secret of printing. He had become embroiled in some financial misadventures that left him unable to repay investors. As a measure of restitution, he supposedly promised to share a secret with his investors, which some believe was the idea of movable-type printing.[9]

Tradition holds that Gutenberg believed his great

invention came as some special insight or inspiration, "like a ray of light."[10] Who can doubt that he was inspired? He seemed to think so. That he believed his work would promote significant good is clear from a famous statement attributed to him: "It is a press, certainly, but a press from which shall flow in inexhaustible streams, the most abundant and most marvelous liquor that has ever flowed to relieve the thirst of man! Through it, God will spread his word. A spring of truth shall flow from it: like a new star it shall scatter the darkness of ignorance, and cause a light heretofore unknown to shine amongst men."[11]

Indeed, Johann Gutenberg's invention not only stimulated increased literacy among lay people in Europe, but it was instrumental in promoting individual freedom and thought as well as increased faith and doctrinal understanding. Gutenberg's masterpiece, and one of the first completed projects off the press, was a two-volume, 42-line, 1,281-page Latin Bible that appeared no later than 1456. It likely required several years of work to produce. The Gutenberg Bible is considered by many as the earliest important printed book in history. An estimated 180 copies of the Bible were produced on both paper and vellum (animal skin); some forty copies of Gutenberg's Bible still exist.[12] These Bibles exude superb craftsmanship and feature hand-done decorations by skilled illuminators.[13] Even before it came off the press, excitement quickly spread about Gutenberg's Bible. Various communiqués, including letters like the following one from an admirer, which dates from March 1455, described Gutenberg's accomplishment:

> All that has been written to me about that marvellous man seen at Frankfurt is true. I have not seen complete Bibles but only a number of quires of various books of the Bible. The script was very neat and legible, not at all difficult to follow—your

grace would be able to read it without effort, and indeed without glasses. . . . I shall try and see if I can have a copy for sale brought here which I can purchase on your behalf. But I fear that won't be possible, both because of the length of the journey and because buyers were said to be lined up even before the books were finished.[14]

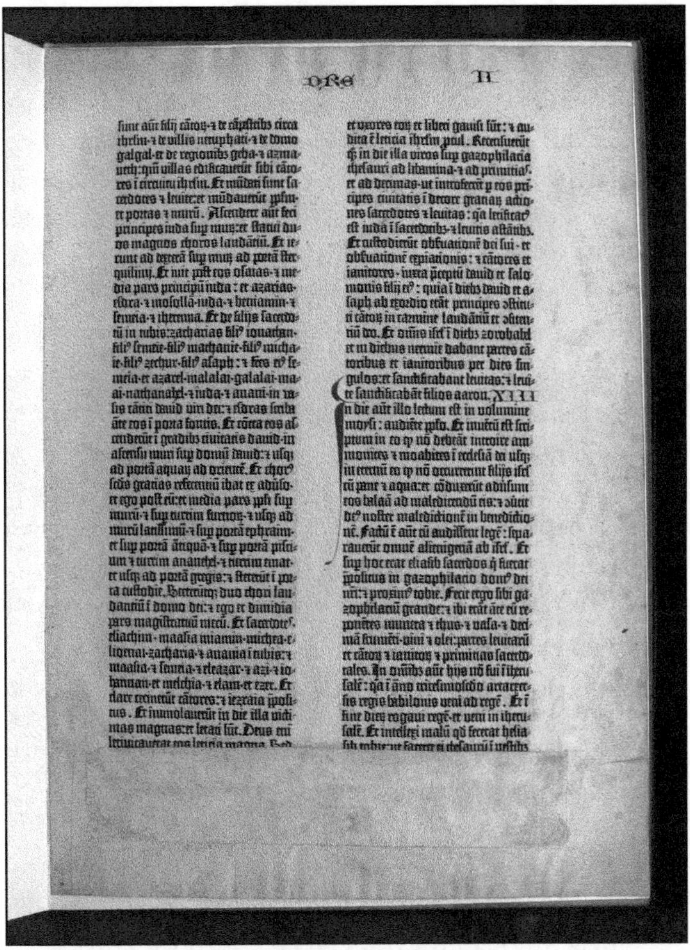

Page from a Gutenberg 42-line Bible (AD 1455).

Though news of Gutenberg's invention spread throughout Europe, he did not get rich, nor was he famous during his lifetime. Curiously, his name does not appear on any of his printed work, not even on the Gutenberg Bible. He apparently was not a very good businessman or promoter, and he was involved in significant lawsuits after a few years following the printing of the Bible. One of these resulted in his forfeiting his main printing equipment to a financial backer, Johann Fust. The amount of unpaid loans and interest claimed by Fust was just over 2,000 guilders. In the fifteenth century this was a large sum of money and would have purchased 250 head of cattle. The court ordered Gutenberg to make the payment. Gutenberg had no choice but to hand over the equipment of his life's work—printing press, metal casts, paper, and other supplies—a heartbreaking sacrifice indeed.[15] Toward the end of his life, Johann left Mainz and moved to Eltville, where he set up another small printing establishment. In addition, the archbishop of Mainz provided an allowance for living expenses, which he kept until his death on February 3, 1468.

Two years after his death, Gutenberg began to receive some of the acclaim he was due. A letter written in December 1470 and printed a year later by the rector of the University of Paris, Professor Guillaume Fichet, describes the inventor's achievement.

> Not far from the city of Mainz there appeared a certain Johann whose surname was Gutenberg, who, first of all men, devised the art of printing, whereby books are made, not by a reed, as did the ancients, nor with a quill pen, as do we, but with metal letters, and that swiftly, neatly, beautifully. Surely this man is worthy to be loaded with divine honors by all the Muses, all the arts, all the tongues of those who delight in books, and is all the more to

> be preferred to gods and goddesses in that he has put the means of choice within reach of letters themselves and of mortals devoted to culture. That great Gutenberg has discovered things far more pleasing and more divine, in carving out letters in such a fashion that whatever can be said or thought can by them be written down at once and transcribed and committed to the memory of posterity.[16]

All this indicates that Johann Gutenberg's destiny was not wealth and glory in mortality. Rather, he seems to have been raised up by God for the specific inventions he made and the work he produced—both of which appeared on the scene at just the right time to revolutionize Christianity and the Western world. In this regard, he is not unlike E. B. Grandin, who was raised up to print the Book of Mormon, and when he had completed his task, his enterprises dwindled. In truth, printing first appeared among the Chinese as early as AD 450. And the first development of movable-type printing was actually seen in Korea a half-century before it appeared in Europe. However, all the evidence indicates that Johann Gutenberg's invention was a totally independent occurrence—a "ray of light," as we said earlier. Elder Bruce R. McConkie said, "Few tools were more effective than printing in paving the way for the great revival of learning, for the religious reformation, and for the breaking away of peoples and nations from religious domination. Without the discovery of movable type in about 1440, the barrier of gross darkness covering the apostate world could scarce have been pierced."[17]

Printing Spreads

Gutenberg's printing methods were used for more than three hundred years after his death, and his invention influenced countless numbers of people. By AD 1500, there were at least

1,700 printing presses in Europe. These had already produced about 20 million volumes of approximately 40,000 different books. Roman Catholic officials worried that more open access to all kinds of written materials would undermine the Church's position. On the other hand, this new accessibility appealed to a great many individuals not worried about the Church's control over men and countries. These included the men and women we now call the Protestant Reformers. Amid the mounting tensions, the Church "hit back."[18] Ultimately, it forbade the printing of anonymous books about religion and also published a list of other forbidden printed materials. "Anything thought likely to encourage the spread of new religious ideas . . . [was] banned."[19] But new ideas could not be stopped. What Gutenberg uncorked was impossible to get back into the genie's bottle.

The first English printer to use Gutenberg's methods was William Caxton. He served as an apprentice to the Lord Mayor of London, went to Bruges, and then to Cologne where he learned the art of printing. In 1476, he returned to London and set up a printing press. Though he did not print any Bibles, "his presses fired the imagination of English reformers," and a new idea burned in their minds: printed Bibles in the vernacular.[20] By the turn of the century, in Wittenberg, Germany, the city of the great Reformer Martin Luther, a printer by the name of Lufft produced more than 100,000 Bibles.[21] This set the stage for the spread of one of the most wrenching conflicts of all time—a conflict that would change the religious, political, and social landscape of the world—the Protestant Reformation.

NOTES

1. Edward P. Cheyney, *The Dawn of a New Era* (New York: Harper Torchbooks, 1962), 212.
2. Ibid, 213.
3. Ibid, 220.

4. John Stevens Kerr, *Ancient Texts Alive Today: The Story of the English Bible*, Charles House, ed. (New York: American Bible Society, 1999), 42.
5. Joseph Fielding Smith, *Doctrines of Salvation*, ed. Bruce R. McConkie (Salt Lake City: Bookcraft, 1956), 1:176, 177, 178
6. *Conference Report*, April 6, 1939, 20.
7. John Man, *Gutenberg: How One Man Remade the World with Words* (New York: John Wiley and Sons), 26–29.
8. "Gutenberg and His Times: Timeline." Gutenberg Museum, Mainz.
9. James Burke, *Connections* (London: Macmillan, 1978), 101–102.
10. James Burke, *The Day the Universe Changed* (Boston: Little, Brown, 1985), 303.
11. ThinkExist.com/quotes/366071.html
12. Kerr, *Ancient Texts Alive Today*, 50.
13. *The Gutenberg Museum—Mainz* (Mainz: Philipp von Zabern, 1998), cover, 10–11, 68–69.
14. Quoted in Martin Davies, *The Gutenberg Bible* (London: The British Library, 1996), 20.
15. Michael Pollard, *Johann Gutenberg, Master of Modern Printing*, (Woodbridge, Connecticut: Blackbirch Press, 2001), 32.
16. James Thorpe, *The Gutenberg Bible* (San Marino, California: Huntington Library, 1999) 30–31.
17. McConkie, *Mormon Doctrine*, 716.
18. Pollard, Johann Gutenberg, 41.
19. Ibid.
20. Connolly, *The Indestructible Book*, 89.
21. Ibid, 88–89.

4.

LUTHER *and* *the* REFORMATION

By 1450, the Roman Catholic Church itself had already realized it was in trouble and had called for reform through its own ecclesiastical councils: Pisa (1409); Constance (1414–1418); and Basel (1431–1449). Adding to the significant challenges already raised by John Wycliffe in England, John Hus in Bohemia, and Girolamo Savonarola in Italy—the most prominent of the pre-Reformation voices—the Church did nothing to curb serious abuses of ecclesiastical power.

Enter Martin Luther (1483–1546), the son of a coalminer in Saxony. Luther's father was a strict disciplinarian, and his mother was a devout practitioner of Catholicism. Luther learned early on that breaking any one of God's commands "would earn a terrible, eternal punishment."[1] His parents taught him about "the little Christ of love and the supreme Christ of judgment," that "Christ sits to judge the living and the dead; He will exact from His people the holy life, and dreadful is His wrath."[2] In secondary literature, Luther's father has been described all the way from wanting only the best for his son to being intensely self-absorbed and completely controlling.

As a young man, Luther went off to boarding school

in Magdeburg, Germany. The school was operated by the pious Brethren of the Common Life. Luther was deeply influenced by their emphasis on simple devotion and righteous living rather than tradition and ritual. The Brethren of the Common Life provided a haven for Luther and others. It is telling that the Brethren "touched and trained more of the leaders of the Reformation period than any other teaching group"—men such as Erasmus, Calvin, and Loyola. The pious and appealing figure of Thomas à Kempis was a Brother of the order.[3]

Luther left Magdeburg for Eisenach (his mother's hometown) to continue his education and then went on to the University of Erfurt—Germany's greatest university at the time—the same university where Johann Gutenberg had attended. Luther completed his undergraduate education at Erfurt after four years, and then earned a master's degree after another two.

Luther's father, Hans, had long held the dream of Martin becoming a lawyer. There was no room for alternatives. So Luther entered law school at Erfurt. Hans even gave him a copy of the expensive legal compendium, *Corpus Juris*. All was right in Hans Luther's world but not in Martin's. Partway into his first year, Martin did an about-face, quit the study of law, and entered the Augustinian monastery in Erfurt to spend the rest of his life (or so he thought) as a monk. The ostensible source of this turnabout was the terror Luther felt when he was nearly struck by lightning and knocked off his horse as he was returning to school one day from his home during a storm. This experience was a tipping point, for it brought into sharp focus his sinfulness—his awful, fallen, wretched state before God. At that moment, he vowed his life to the monastic calling.

In truth, this turn of events was not as sudden as it might seem at first blush. The lightning storm brought to the forefront feelings that had been percolating just beneath the surface for some time. Luther had always been somewhat anxious about the welfare of his eternal soul. In a way, he could not help it, given his upbringing. His brush with death demanded that he do something about his spiritual state.

Hans Luther was both heartbroken and furious over his son's deviation from the chosen path. For many months, the severe rift between father and son seemed to be permanent. Though the elder Luther finally acknowledged his son's choice, he never got over it.

Once he was settled into the monastic routine, Luther began concentrating on the next battle—the eradication of the characteristics of the flesh. He intensified, even redoubled, his efforts at living a life of extreme piety but found no relief. He fasted until he had no strength. He locked himself in his unheated cell and prayed until exhaustion overcame him.[4] Still, the terror over his standing before God persisted. The one bright spot in his life was scripture.

The Bible had always played an important role in Luther's life, but now it became an anchor to all of his activity. Biblical study was the respite in the daily challenge of monastic life that he had chosen for himself.[5] In the monastery at Erfurt, Luther immersed himself in the Bible. It provided a happy counterbalance to the anxiety that kept plaguing him over his spiritual condition. When he entered the order of Augustinian Friars, Martin had been given a red-bound Latin Bible for his personal use. It was "precious to him."[6] He studied it so thoroughly he could quote huge passages by heart. The Bible became a major part of his thinking, and he began to use it as a criterion for all judgments. "He read it long and carefully, grounding himself in it with intense, imaginative eagerness. What came later to [be] public expression in his lectures at the University of

Wittenberg had its beginnings [at Erfurt]. His mind and heart found great refreshment in the exhaustless well."[7]

There arose a time when it looked as though Luther might be cut off from the wellspring of spiritual sustenance. One of his teachers, Dr. Usingen, was greatly disturbed by Luther's constant intellectual activity directly involving the Bible, and he told him to leave it alone. "What is the Bible?" Usingen asked. "It is better to read the old doctors who have drawn the truth from the Bible. The Bible is the cause of all sedition."[8] Of course, this assessment was precisely the perspective of the medieval Church. But in the views of men like Wycliffe, Hus, and others, what else could the hierarchy expect except sedition when the precepts they promulgated had strayed so far from biblical principles? The only thing they could do was keep the Bible away from everyone except those in positions to perpetuate the errors.

In 1508, Luther was transferred to the monastery at Wittenberg, where, the following year, he was awarded the degree of Doctor of Theology and continued his thorough immersion in the Bible. He became a professor of biblical literature. Wittenberg would be his home until his death in 1546.[9]

Ultimately, Johann von Staupitz was the man most responsible for Luther's rebirth. He was not only vicar-general of the Saxon province, where Luther lived, but he was also dean of the faculty of theology at the University of Wittenberg. Von Staupitz took a special interest in Luther as he watched the inner struggle of the young friar. Von Staupitz not only revoked the prohibition against studying the Bible but also gave Luther the counsel that changed his life yet again. His gentle but direct advice, keen insight, and sympathetic manner helped complete Luther's change of mind and heart. Von Staupitz's greatest instruction was never forgotten by Luther: "Look not on your own imaginary sins, but look at Christ crucified, where your real sins are forgiven, and hold with deep courage to God."[10] At this point, Luther's life became centered wholly on the Bible, which revealed the "true" Christ.

Though the months came and went and Luther still had feelings that God was angry at him for his sins, his outlook gradually began to change. On the advice of his supervisor, he studied the writings of St. Paul, St. Augustine, and Bernard of Clairvaux. Through his association with them, the doctrine of God's free grace in Christ came to occupy his thoughts. He became convinced that only the Lord's grace and mercy could rescue him. He always turned to scripture to find confirmation of the ideas found in St. Augustine, and he found it. A new conception of Christ formed in his heart. Even the terror and damnation he felt over the doctrine of predestination, of which Augustine was also the master articulator, began to lose its grip. (Augustine was the namesake of Luther's monastic order.)

As Luther worked on his doctoral degree, his trust in the doctrine of God's grace grew stronger. But the event that truly completed his conversion occurred in 1510 while in Rome as a member of a delegation to the papal curia (court). In the holy city, his soul thrilled as he visited shrines and churches. But when he went to the great sacred stairs of the St. John Lateran Church, which led to a room filled with relics of the saints, the now-famous episode involving the text of Romans 1:17 occurred. While climbing the steps known as Sancta Scala on his knees (having been told that such an act would earn him a year's indulgence), the words of Romans 1:17 kept echoing in his ears. "What folly," he thought, "to seek indulgence from the Church for my acts when God is willing to acquit me of my sins if I believe in His Son."[11]

"Seventy-two years after Luther climbed as a penitent

these stairs, his son Paul said he had heard his father tell how in the midst of the climb he recalled the text, 'The just shall live by faith,' and walked back down."[12] No fanfare, but great change!

Luther left Rome a different person. Simple faith in Christ was the true path to salvation, not a multiplicity of good works, not the Church sacraments or rituals. Each person was answerable to God directly—not through priestly intermediaries. God justifies human beings through his love, meaning that God puts individuals in a right relationship with Him by imparting to them the righteousness of Jesus Christ through His atoning sacrifice.

This became the heart of Luther's teaching, and it was grounded in scripture. His theology contradicted accepted Church doctrine, but that didn't matter. For Luther, the Bible was the sole authority in matters of faith and doctrine. That is why it is sometimes said that the Bible is, in a sense, a Protestant book.[13]

Religious Revolution

The trigger for the opening events of the Protestant Reformation was the arrival one day of Johann Tetzel selling indulgences in the vicinity of Wittenberg. According to the doctrine of indulgences, Jesus Christ and the saints of past ages had performed such good works while alive that they accumulated an excess of merit in the heavenly treasury, which the Pope could apply to the credit of penitent sinners once this excess merit had been purchased by individuals for themselves or loved ones. This excess merit, once applied, shortened an individual's stay in purgatory. By the sixteenth century, this concept had become little more than a grand money-making scheme. Huge sums flowed into Church coffers from all over Europe. The more inventive representatives of the Pope even applied catchy slogans to their enterprise, such as this well-known ditty:

"once a coin in the coffer sings, a soul from purgatory springs."

In response to Tetzel's crass merchandising of sacred things, Luther posted his famous Ninety-Five Theses (propositions) on the door of the Castle Church in Wittenberg on 31 October 1517. He proposed to debate the doctrine of indulgences, as well as other tenets (and abuses), in public. Luther did not start out to rend the Church nor to break away from it as a declared heretic. In fact, biographies of Luther mention his surprise and dismay over being thrust into the limelight and cast as a national hero. He found support among political rulers and like-minded churchmen. Only when he realized that his position was irreconcilable with the Church's stance did he make a clean, clear, and unequivocal break with the Roman Catholic Church. He then began publishing a series of pamphlets that vigorously denounced the Pope and the pervasive corruption in the Church. He called upon the German princes of the Empire to take control of Church property (a long-recognized factor in contributing to the venality of a rich and worldly organization). He called for these rulers to set themselves up as heads of the Christian Church in Germany. From this call developed the adage, *cuious regio eious religio* ("Who rules the region rules the religion").

At first the Pope did not take Luther or his burgeoning revolution seriously, referring to Luther as a drunken monk who would sober up and "a wild boar which has invaded the Lord's vineyard."[14] But that soon changed. In January 1521, Pope Leo X excommunicated Luther and officially declared him a heretic. A few months later, in April, Emperor Charles V summoned Luther to appear before an official diet (legislative assembly) of the Holy Roman Empire at Worms in Germany. By then Luther was so famous that crowds gathered to get a glimpse of "the revolutionary" and observe

Castle Church in Wittenburg, Germany, where the Protestant Reformation "began."

the spectacle. At six o'clock in the evening of Wednesday, April 17, Luther was ushered into the bishop's palace and the meeting of the diet. Charles V was there along with six electors of the Empire, including Luther's own civil lord, Elector Frederick; papal legates; Dr. Johann Eck, Vice-Chancellor of the University of Ingoldstadt, who conducted the proceedings; and "thousands of persons jammed into the passageways and doors."[15]

After two days of verbal exchange, including Luther's request for more time to prepare his response to the matter of recanting, the moment arrived that remains forever framed in the annals of history like a timeless photograph.

> Dr. Eck: "Luther, you have not answered the point. . . . Will you recant or not?
>
> Dr. Luther: "Since your Majesty and your lordships ask for a plain answer, I will give you one without either horns or teeth. Unless I am convinced by Scripture or by right reason—for I trust neither in Popes nor in councils, since they have often erred and contradicted themselves—unless I am thus convinced, I am bound by the texts of the Bible; my conscience is captive to the Word of God. I neither can nor will recant anything, since it is neither right nor safe to act against conscience. God help me. Amen."[16]

The point was sharply defined, not just for the diet, but for all posterity. The Bible was at the heart of one of the greatest revolutions in history. There could be no wavering on the point of biblical authority.

Luther's German Translation

Because the Bible was the sole authoritative source of Christian dogma in Luther's view, he realized that all the German people needed to have access to the scriptures, which necessitated a reliable translation into German. Luther began his translation shortly after the legislative assembly ended. As he returned home from Worms on May 4, 1521, he was captured in the Thuringian forest by men he thought were some thugs of the Church, but who turned out to be in the employ of the Elector Frederick, protector of the heretic. Luther was taken to Wartburg Castle where his identity was kept secret. There he prepared manuscripts for a German edition of the New Testament. He worked from Erasmus's second edition of the New Testament in Greek, the original language of the New Testament. Luther's translation was done in such excellent style that it became a standard in helping to establish modern literary German.

Earlier German Bibles were in existence at the time Luther made his translation, the latest being a revised edition (1483) of an anonymous version first made in Strasbourg in 1466. As one authority notes, however, "[The revised Strasbourg text] had been adapted directly and uncritically from the Vulgate and its stilted sentences often emerge into the German language as endearingly quaint and incomprehensible as many of those in the earlier version of the Wycliffite Bible. Luther discarded all this. He must have known the German versions current in his own time but there is not a hint of them in his new translation. Luther was fluent in Latin and Greek and competent in Hebrew. He took with him to Wartburg [Castle] a copy of the second edition of the *Novum Instrumentum* (1519), and he began to translate directly from the original Greek in [that] edition of Erasmus."[17]

Luther himself referred to the room of the Wartburg Castle where he did his translating as his Patmos (a reference to the Apostle John's habitat of exile where he recorded the book of Revelation). Typical of Luther's thoroughness, he went back to Wittenberg in March 1522 (at the peril of his life) with the manuscript translation of the New Testament and went over it, sentence by sentence, with his friend and fellow reformer, Philip Melanchthon.[18] The new translation came off the printing press on September 21, 1522 (a day of the month of interest to Latter-day Saints). Luther regarded some books of the New Testament—Hebrews, James, Jude, and Revelation—as non-canonical and therefore placed them at the end of his German translation.

After finishing the New Testament, Luther began work-

The room in Wartburg Castle where Luther prepared his German edition of the New Testament.

ing on a German translation of the Hebrew Old Testament. He completed this translation years later. In all, Luther's German translations of the two testaments have gone

An illustrated page from Luther's 1525 Bible—the sacrifice of Abraham.

through some 377 editions, thanks to Gutenberg's invention. Though the King James Version of the Bible does not trace its history directly to Luther's translation, the Luther Bible is nonetheless significant, being among the first of the new vernacular translations to come from the original-language texts of the Bible. It influenced later translations of the English Bible, including William Tyndale's, to which the King James Version does trace its history.

The German Bible also had a significant connection to the Restoration. At one point, the Prophet Joseph Smith indicated he possessed old editions of the New Testament in different languages. "I have been reading the German," he said, "and find it to be the most [nearly] correct translation and to correspond nearest to the revelations which God has given to me for the last fourteen years."[19] Our doctrinal understanding today is not without a German tie.

Conclusion

Who can doubt that the Spirit of the Lord influenced Luther's activities in general, and his inspiring response at the Diet of Worms in particular? We need only be reminded of the convictions of many modern Latter-day Saint leaders that Martin Luther was one of the foreordained, prepared, and inspired forerunners to the Restoration as well as to the King James Version of the Bible. He was courageous beyond belief and was willing to sacrifice everything for what he believed to be the truth.

In the same month that Luther was transported to Wartburg Castle, Emperor Charles V signed the Edict of Worms, a document that essentially put out a contract on Luther's life. The Edict declared Luther to be an outlaw of the Empire and granted permission for anyone to kill him without fear of prosecution. Because of Elector Frederick's protection, Luther continued to function as the informal leader of the Protestant movement until his death in 1546.

His reforms included the abolishment of the Church hierarchy of Popes, cardinals, and bishops. He proclaimed that the Church was made up of a priesthood of all believers. He kept only two of the seven sacraments of the Roman Catholic Church because only they were supported by the Bible: baptism and the Eucharist (or the Lord's Supper). Like Wycliffe before him, Luther rejected transubstantiation—again because it could not be supported from scripture.

Bust of Martin Luther in Erfurt, Germany.

Finally, Luther's reforms had a profound affect on marriage and family life. He abolished celibacy and married a former nun, Katherine von Bora (Katey, as he called her), with whom he had six children, three boys and three girls. He supported orphaned relatives as well. As one authority noted:

> Luther married with a clear expectation of the difficulties to follow. He was not prepared for the strange, quiet happiness that slowly came into his life as their home settled into a normal routine.

> Katherine brought to him a strong and willing service, a loyal and sympathetic heart, and a keen and delightful sense of humor. She was increasingly a source of joy and peace to him for the rest of his life. The highest tribute he ever paid her was when he spoke one day of St. Paul's Epistle to the Romans: 'This is my Catharine von Bora.' In the Epistle to the Romans, Luther's heart first had found its religious peace.[20]

Paul's letter to the Romans was the initial source of true peace in his life. Because of life with his Katey, Luther enjoyed the culmination of that peace. Indeed, he came to know God more fully with her at his side, as well as the truth of God's wisdom, it is not good for man to be alone.

Notes

1. Several histories have been consulted. See especially Edwin P. Booth, *Martin Luther: Heart of the Reformation*, ed. Dan Harmon (Uhrichsville, OH: Barbour, 2003), 10.
2. Ibid.
3. Ibid, 17.
4. Ibid, 33–34.
5. See the assessment in G. A. Nielson, *Twelve Reformation Heroes* (Belfast: Ambassador Publications; Greenville, SC: Emerald House, n.d.), 29–30.
6. Booth, *Martin Luther*, 42.
7. Ibid.
8. Ibid.
9. Ibid, 17–64.
10. Ibid, 50.
11. Nielson, *Twelve Reformation Heroes*, 31.
12. Booth, *Martin Luther*, 60.

13. See, for example, Benson Bobrick, *Wide as the Waters* (New York: Simon and Schuster, 2001), 16.
14. Barbara W. Tuchman, *The March of Folly* (New York: Ballantine Books, 1984), 116.
15. The scene is engagingly told in Booth, *Martin Luther*, 113–14.
16. Quoted in Booth, *Martin Luther*, 123.
17. Christopher D. Hamel, *The Book. A History of the Bible* (London: Phaidon Press Limited, 2001), 229.
18. Hamel, *The Book*, 229.
19. Joseph Smith, *Teachings of the Prophet Joseph Smith*, 349.
20. Booth, *Martin Luther*, 163–64.

5.

The Renaissance *and the* Reformation

The Reformation did not occur in a vacuum. The European cultural movement known as the Renaissance ("rebirth") not only supported these monumental changes, but in many ways it was responsible for precipitating the religious revolution brought to a head by Martin Luther and his associates. Lasting roughly from AD 1300 to 1600 and beginning mainly in Italy, the Renaissance was also known as the revival of antiquity or revival of learning, in contrast to the Middle Ages (AD 300–1300). It was a period of renewed interest in and intense study of the culture and languages of classical antiquity, Greek and Roman.

Humanism has been called the *philosophy* of the Renaissance, but humanism was in some ways also the *methodology* of the Renaissance. Renaissance humanists believed that classical antiquity should be studied in order to understand how the civilizations of Greece and Rome served as models for the cultures and people of the new age in which they believed they were living. Humanists first had to master the Greek and Latin languages and texts of antiquity. Renaissance scholars in Northern Europe, known as Christian Humanists, were interested in the humanistic method, especially understanding Greek and

Latin, in order to study original Christianity and, in particular, the premier ancient text on which Christianity was founded, the Bible. Christianity was also part of Greek and Roman culture.

Perhaps the leading Christian Humanist was Desiderius Erasmus (1466–1536). He played an important role in both the early history of the Reformation and the history of biblical translations. He, like his younger contemporary, Luther, courageously refused to abandon his ideals. To him goes the honor of preparing the first accessible Greek New Testament in 1516. Erasmus' Greek New Testament was the edition on which many subsequent versions of the Bible were based, especially the English.

Erasmus was born in Rotterdam as the illegitimate son of a monk. He was destined to become known as one of the keenest minds of Christian Humanism, but his was not a life of ease. At age eight, he went to the school of the Brethren of the Common Life—the training ground for many key players of the Reformation. At age eleven, he suffered the loss of both parents (who had subsequently married) to the plague. Though desiring to remain free from controlling people and organizations, he was forced to join an Augustinian monastery owing to his destitute condition. Eventually he left the monastery to become secretary to a prominent bishop. He entered the greatest phase of his life after an old schoolmaster encouraged the bishop to allow Erasmus to study at the University of Paris—one of Europe's most prestigious educational institutions.[1]

Erasmus's life was hard—one of solitude and precarious subsistence. To supplement his meager income, Erasmus learned and subsequently taught Greek. This was possible owing to the increased interest in classical antiquity, to be sure, but it was also a function of the increased availability of Greek manuscripts and books in both institutional libraries at the great universities of Europe as well as those of princes and private persons. This, in turn, was "accelerated by the development of the printing press and the growth of a lay reading public."[2] One of Erasmus's students, William Blount, persuaded Erasmus to go to England and study Greek at Oxford University. While there, he met and became lifelong friends with some of the future luminaries of the age—Dr. John Colet (who lectured on the book of Romans at Oxford), Thomas More, and the young future king, Henry VIII. Because of his dazzling mind and popular writings, he was afforded the opportunity to travel to Rome and Venice. At the University of Turin he was awarded a doctorate. In 1505, back in England, he wrote his most famous work, a satire entitled *In Praise of Folly*, wherein he described the Popes, bishops, kings, and princes of Europe being enslaved by the personification of Folly.

In 1510, Erasmus went to Cambridge University to teach. He had long desired to make a critical edition of the Latin Vulgate when a Swiss printer requested he make an edition of the New Testament in Greek. Believing that good theology was the offspring of a good knowledge of grammar, Erasmus agreed to the new project.[3] He went to Basel, Switzerland, in 1515 to do the work. Aware that Cardinal Francisco Ximenes de Cisneros (1437–1517) was working on the first Polyglot Bible, Erasmus rushed his New Testament to completion in ten months (1516).

In 1502, Cardinal Ximenes had conceived of a carefully prepared Bible arranged in four parallel columns of text: Hebrew, Aramaic (various targums), Greek, and Latin. It is called the *Complutensian Polyglot*.[4]

The Polyglot New Testament was actually printed in 1514, but Erasmus's Greek text was distributed before Ximenes's monumental work. However, haste resulted in hundreds of errors in Erasmus' edition. Even Erasmus later admitted that his work was "precipitated rather than edited" (*praecipitatum verius quam editum*).[5] For example, to establish the text of Revelation, Erasmus borrowed a twelfth-century Greek manuscript of that book from his friend and fellow scholar, Johannes Reuchlin. In addition to the fact that the manuscript was almost impossible to read in places, it was missing the last page. So Erasmus took the Vulgate and translated the last six verses back into Greek to finish his edition.[6]

All of the quirks and errors did not seem to diminish the magnitude of Erasmus's achievement. Though the work of Cardinal Ximenes and his editor, Stunica, was indisputably better, Erasmus's edition was the more popular of the two. When it was first made available to the public and Stunica brought its deficiencies to the attention of Ximenes, the magnanimous old cardinal replied, "Would God that all the Lord's people were prophets! Produce better, if thou canst; condemn not the industry of another."[7] This language will resonate with Latter-day Saints because of what the Lord said to the early elders of this dispensation. You are justified in criticizing the Book of Commandments if you can "make one like unto it" (D&C 67:7).

One of the truly problematic passages in Erasmus' Greek New Testament has both an interesting history and significant implications for the Latter-day Saint doctrine of the Godhead. This is 1 John 5:7–8, which scholars have labeled the Johannine Comma. In the Latin Vulgate, the passage reads: "There are three that bear witness in heaven: the Father, the Word, and the Spirit, and these three are one; and there are three that bear witness on earth, the Spirit, the water, and the blood, and these three are one."[8] The significance of these verses is that they constitute "the only passage in the entire Bible that explicitly delineates the doctrine of the Trinity"[9] as proclaimed by most Christian denominations—the idea that the Father, Son, and Holy Ghost are one triune God.

The problem is that the wording of the Latin Vulgate is not attested in most of the Greek manuscripts of the New Testament, nor in the Greek manuscripts on which Erasmus based his edition. Therein the passage simply reads: "There are three that bear witness: the Spirit, the water, and the blood, and these three are one." Therefore, Erasmus did not originally include in his edition of the Greek New Testament the extra words of the Latin version: " . . . in heaven: the Father, the Word, and the Spirit, and these three are one; and there are three that bear witness on earth . . ." Erasmus believed in being true to the original texts. And he was, therefore, an advocate of Church reform. He would have agreed with Wycliffe's belief in biblical authority—but adding a detail: if it is not found in the *earliest* texts of the Bible, it is not authentic.

The repercussions of Erasmus' omission are explained by a modern New Testament authority:

> More than anything else, it was this that outraged the theologians of his day, who accused Erasmus of tampering with the text in an attempt to eliminate the doctrine of the Trinity and to devalue its corollary, the doctrine of the full divinity of Christ. In particular, Stunica, one of the chief editors of the Complutensian Polyglot, went public with his defamation of Erasmus and insisted that in future editions he return the verse to its rightful place.
>
> As the story goes, Erasmus—possibly in an unguarded moment—agreed that he would insert the verse in a future edition of his Greek New Testament on one condition; that his opponents produce a Greek manuscript in which the verse could be found (finding it in Latin manuscripts was

> not enough). And so a Greek manuscript was produced. In fact, it was produced for the occasion. It appears that someone copied out the Greek text of the Epistles, and when he came to the passage in question, he translated the Latin text [back] into Greek, giving the Johannine Comma in its familiar, theologically useful form. The manuscript provided to Erasmus, in other words, was a sixteenth-century production, made to order.
>
> Despite his misgivings, Erasmus was true to his word and included the Johannine Comma in his next edition, and in all his subsequent editions. . . . These editions provided the form of the text that the translators of the King James Bible eventually used.[10]

Erasmus's first edition of the Greek New Testament with accompanying Latin translation was printed on 672 pages. To assure its acceptance, he dedicated it to Pope Leo X. But he also captured the spirit of the Reformers, both before and after him, in the words he wrote in its preface: "I do not at all share the opinion of those who do not want laymen to read the Sacred Scriptures in the vernacular, as though Christ had taught something enigmatic to be scarcely understood by a few theologians. They seem to think that the Christian religion is best protected by ignorance. I wish all women would read the Gospels and the letters of Paul. I wish they would be translated into all the languages. I wish the peasants would sing them behind the plough, the weaver at his loom, the pilgrim on his way."[11]

Erasmus's Greek New Testament went through five editions (1516, 1519, 1522, 1527, and 1535). About 3,300 copies of the first two editions were printed.[12] It is generally conceded that the fourth edition is the definitive work. It contains three parallel columns: Erasmus's Greek text, the

Latin Vulgate, and Erasmus's own Latin translation of the Greek. He corrected typographical errors and used Cardinal Ximenes's *Complutensian Polyglot* to fix problems in his previous editions.

Conclusion

It would be hard to overestimate the effect of Martin Luther on history. He is a towering, monumental figure. That is obvious to almost all persons who know anything about the modern world. It is much easier to overlook the contributions and significance of Desiderius Erasmus. Nonetheless, he is also a towering figure in the general history of Western civilization and the narrower field of Bible translation, especially with regard to the history of the English Bible. Erasmus's work of 1516 was the first time the New Testament was made generally available in the original language of that testament.

Erasmus's editions of the Greek New Testament formed the basis of vernacular translations of the New Testament throughout much of Europe. Reformers and Bible translators used his New Testament for many years after its appearance. Martin Luther used the second edition (1519) to give to the German peoples a Bible in their own tongue—a Bible which set the standard for the German language, unified the German people, and changed the theological landscape of the world, which we still feel today. William Tyndale undoubtedly used Erasmus's third edition to give the people of England, and the world, a superior version of the New Testament in English. Tyndale's Bible, in turn, set a standard for the English language, influenced Shakespeare, and literally formed the foundation of the King James Version (a huge percentage of the King James Version being taken directly from Tyndale). The fourth and fifth editions of Erasmus's Greek New Testament were also used in the process of printing the King James Version. Last, but not least,

Ulrich Zwingli and John Calvin used the Erasmus New Testament to translate a Bible into the vernacular of their peoples.

Ultimately, we cannot help but believe that the Lord's hand was upon both Luther and Erasmus. One separated from the Roman Catholic Church, and the other did not. One argued that the papacy was corrupt, the other argued that it was improper to speak evil of the Pope in public. But both men were honorable and true to their convictions. Both men cherished the New Testament and knew the text better, perhaps, than any other two of their age. Both revered Jesus Christ. In the end, both saw the need and worked for a reformed ecclesiastical institution. As Erasmus himself admitted, he "laid the egg which Luther hatched."[13] And it is not difficult to see why Latter-day Saint prophetic voices credited the Renaissance with being part of God's plan as it led to the Restoration in the nineteenth century. President Joseph Fielding Smith stated explicitly that the Renaissance prepared the way for the Restoration.[14] Renaissance, Reformation, and Restoration were all part of God's sweeping vision for his children.

Notes

1. Connolly, *The Indestructible Book* (Grand Rapids, MI: Baker Books, 1996), 89–90.
2. Myron P. Gilmore, *The World of Humanism*, 1453–1517 (New York: Harper Torchbooks, 1962), 186.
3. Paul D. Wegner, *The Journey from Texts to Translations* (Grand Rapids, MI: Baker Academic, 2000), 267.
4. Work on the polyglot was done in Alcala, Spain, called Complutum in Latin. Hence the name of the Bible. Wegner, *Journey from Texts to Translations*, 266.
5. See Bart D. Ehrman, *Misquoting Jesus: The Story Behind Who Changed the Bible and Why* (New York:

HarperSanFrancisco, 2005), 79. He translates the Latin phrase as "rushed out rather than edited."

6. Ehrman, *Misquoting Jesus*, 78–79.
7. Quoted in Wegner, *Journey from Texts to Translations*, 267.
8. Ehrman, *Misquoting Jesus*, 81.
9. Ibid, 81.
10. Ibid, 81–82.
11. *Novum Testamentum* (Basel, 1516). Quoted in the excellent source book by Hans J. Hillerbrand, *The Reformation: A Narrative History Related by Contemporary Observers and Participants* (New York: Harper and Row, 1964), 423.
12. Connolly, *The Indestructible Book*, 90.
13. Ibid, 91.
14. Joseph Fielding Smith, *Doctrines of Salvation*, ed. Bruce R. McConkie (Salt Lake City: Bookcraft, 1956), 1:176–177.

6.

The Ploughboy's Educator: William Tyndale

A little more than a century passed between the death of John Wycliffe in 1384 and the coming of a man the world would recognize as the "Father of the English Bible"—William Tyndale. By the time Tyndale turned his considerable intellectual prowess to a new and improved version of the Bible in English, Luther and Erasmus were already working for reform. Gutenberg had printed his now-famous 42-line Bible, inaugurated a new information age, and passed off the world's stage. Not least, individuals living in and out of England had become well-acquainted with Wycliffe's first English Bible and taken up the cause to make the scriptures the center of Christian theology.

Even the threat of Church punishment—languishing in a dank prison cell or being consumed by agonizing fires at the stake—could not intimidate or dissuade these courageous souls from studying the word of God directly from the source. A set of laws called the Constitutions of Oxford of 1407–09 forbade the owning or making of English translations of the Bible, and yet, "men and women were still being burned alive for the possession of such 'Lollard' material well over a hundred years later."[1] However, an increasingly greater challenge developed for English Bible readers: navigating the difficult and stilted translation left by Wycliffe and his collaborators. For those living in the English realm, the Latin recitations of Church liturgy and ritual, as well as the Latin text of the Bible being read to them, rendered religious experience all but incomprehensible.

Europe was thus poised on the brink of something new and wonderful, and the convergence of these amazing circumstances seemed to cry out for the appearance of a true hero and towering genius the likes of Master Tyndale. His courage and sacrifice were exceeded only by his linguistic abilities. His work went directly into the King James Bible published a little more than a hundred years (1611) after his birth. "Through that King James Bible, which dominated the English-speaking world for 350 years, Tyndale has reached more people than Shakespeare."[2] It is not an exaggeration to say that, in part, the Restoration of the gospel of Jesus Christ is a product of William Tyndale. God raised him up at the exact moment he was needed.

Early Preparation

William Tyndale was born sometime between 1490 and 1495 to an affluent farming family in Gloucestershire, England, overlooking the hills of Wales. He went off to Oxford University at age twelve and had completed a master of arts degree by 1515—also the year of his ordination. He became fluent in eight languages: English, German, French, Spanish, Italian, Greek, Hebrew, and Latin.[3] The sixteenth-century historian John Foxe described him as a thoroughgoing product of Oxford (like Wycliffe before him) and one who was "addicted" to the scriptures.

> [Tyndale was] brought up from a child in the University of Oxford, where he, by long continuance, increased as well in the knowledge of

> tongues, and other liberal arts, as especially in the knowledge of the Scriptures, whereunto his mind was singularly addicted; insomuch that he, lying then in Magdalen hall, read privily to certain students and fellows of Magdalen college some parcel of divinity; instructing them in the knowledge and truth of the Scriptures. His manners and conversation being correspondent to the same, were such, that all they had knew him, reputed him to be a man of most virtuous disposition, and of life unspotted.[4]

Oxford University, where William Tyndale lived and completed his master of arts degree.

Surely it was Tyndale's virtue and purity that allowed him to be the vessel through which God could work. After teaching at Oxford for a time, he moved to Cambridge, where he "likewise made his abode a certain space [b]eing now further ripened in the knowledge of God's Word."[5] There he also came in contact with new theological ideas promoted by scholars who supported Church reform, including Miles

Coverdale, John Frith, and Thomas Bilney. Luther's writings were, as we might say, served up as sumptuous fare for their "theological feasts." Moreover, not only was Cambridge at that time "a centre of aggressive Lutheranism," but it seems just before Tyndale was there, "the Lady Margaret's Professor of Divinity had been Erasmus himself, teaching Greek to, as he admitted, bored undergraduates."[6] We know this impacted Tyndale, for when he returned to Gloucestershire, he had with him Erasmus's new translation of the New Testament from the original Greek, the *Novum Instrumentum* of 1516.

Back in Gloucestershire, Tyndale tutored the children of a notable nobleman, Sir John Walsh, and served as his chaplain. Fearlessly, Master William entered into spirited discussions of the day on theology with various clergy and visitors to Little Sodbury Manor, which often took place around the Walsh's dinner table, as John Foxe describes:

> [T]here resorted to him [Walsh] many times sundry abbots, deans, archdeacons, with divers other doctors, and great beneficed men; who there, together with Master Tyndale sitting at the same table, did use many times to enter communication, and talk of learned men, as of Luther and of Erasmus; also of divers other controversies and questions upon the Scripture.
>
> Then Master Tyndale, as he was learned and well practiced in God's matters, spared not to show unto them simply and plainly his judgment, and when they at any time did vary from Tyndale in opinions, he would show them in the Book, and lay plainly before them the open and manifest places of the Scriptures, to confute their errors and confirm his sayings. And thus continued they for a certain season, reasoning and contending together divers

> times, till at length they waxed weary, and bare a secret grudge in their hearts against him.[7]

It is at this juncture we see Tyndale's views on the importance of the Bible as the yardstick of Church doctrine and practice come into clearer focus. And we also see opponents beginning to rise up to thwart Tyndale. On one occasion, Tyndale was summoned to the residence of a Church leader to answer charges of heresy instigated by one who bore "a secret grudge" against him resulting from the Walsh dinner table conversations. Although treated "as though he had been a dog,"[8] Tyndale could not be moved from positions he knew were right. Truth was more important than his pride or his safety. Fortunately, nothing came of the mini-inquisition except maybe the solidification of Tyndale's views regarding the importance of the Bible and people's access to it. On another occasion, Master William had his now-famous encounter with the "learned man" who stated the Church-supported view that people were better off to be without God's law found in scripture than without the Pope's. "Master Tyndale hearing that, answered him, I defy the Pope and all his laws, and said, if God spare my life ere many years, I will cause a boy that driveth the plough, shall know more of scripture than thou dost."[9]

The die was cast. Master William possessed a conviction that he must provide for the "ploughboy's" education by producing a reliable, readable edition of the Bible in English. Individuals in England needed access to the scriptures in order to withstand errors promulgated by Church leaders. The laity deserved better than to be at the mercy of priests who tried to discredit teachings that Tyndale knew were true. Said he:

> I had perceived by experience how that it was impossible to establish the lay people in any truth,

> except the scripture were plainly laid before their eyes in their mother tongue, that they might see the process, order and the meaning of the text.[10]
>
> If [English] Christians possessed the Holy Scriptures in their own tongue, they could of themselves withstand these attacks. Without the Bible it is impossible to establish the people in truth. . . . Christians must read the New Testament [for themselves] in their own tongue.[11]

Work Begins

Tyndale knew he needed solid support, both financial and ecclesiastical, for such an ambitious project as a new edition of the Bible in English. He had started translating the Bible in his small attic room at Little Sodbury Manor, but he realized he was endangering the lives of the Walsh family by doing so under their roof. Just two years before, "six men and one woman had been burned to death in Coventry for teaching their children to recite the Lord's Prayer in English."[12] Therefore, in 1523, at about the age of thirty, he went to London to ask the Bishop of London, Cuthbert Tunstall, for permission and help to carry out his dream. This was actually a shrewd move on Tyndale's part, for Bishop Tunstall was a scholar (fellow Oxonian), a friend of Erasmus, and a forward-looking churchman—or so Tyndale thought. Tunstall coolly rebuffed the request,[13] apparently fearing that a Bible for the common people in England would fan the fires of religious revolt started by Luther, who by then had been excommunicated two years. This rejection sparked an epiphany, causing Tyndale to realize that not only was there no room in the bishop's palace to translate the New Testament, "there was no place to do it in all England."[14]

In 1524, with the help of a wealthy cloth merchant named

Humphrey Monmouth, Tyndale left England—never to see it again—and moved to Hamburg, Germany. He believed he was on God's errand. He made his way to Wittenberg, where Luther had posted his Ninety-five Theses, and got caught up in the discussion of Luther's doctrine of justification by faith alone. He met fellow Englishman, William Roye, a linguist who assisted Tyndale in finishing his translation of Erasmus's Greek New Testament into English in August 1525. They went to Cologne and found a printer, Peter Quentel. Why they chose Cologne remains unclear, as it was a very conservative center of Catholicism. Unfortunately, Roye was an indiscrete braggart, especially after he had imbibed a few beers. Perhaps he was the one responsible for tipping off Johannes Cochlaeus in an unguarded moment about Tyndale's secret project. Cochlaeus was an enemy of Reformation and alerted the authorities, who then shut down the printing operation. Only Matthew's Gospel and

A Tyndale Pentateuch (AD 1530) containing an illustration of William Tyndale. It is only one of two known copies.

part of Mark had been finished. But Tyndale gathered up the completed sections, fled to Worms in Germany, and was finally able to get the complete New Testament printed by printer Peter Schoeffer.[15]

Several thousand copies of the new master work were smuggled into England in barrels of flour and bolts of cloth. Humphrey Monmouth and his underground book-selling operation helped distribute the copies. Tyndale's New Testament became an immediate bestseller. People were hungry for the word of God. Between 1525 and 1528, 18,000 copies were sold, which was no small feat. Sponsoring merchants priced each copy at half a crown or two-and-one-half shillings. To provide perspective, it would have cost a stone mason five days' wages to purchase a Tyndale New Testament (the equivalent of about $500 in today's economy).[16] Can modern readers appreciate what it cost our predecessors to possess the word of God? Can we appreciate the treasure we sometimes take for granted?

Tyndale's Bibles fomented national unrest. Bishop Tunstall was enraged. King Henry VIII, not yet a Protestant, was angry. It should be remembered that this was eight years before Henry broke away from the Catholic Church over the issue of divorcing his first wife, Katherine. Johannes Cochlaeus, who had prevented the printing of Tyndale's New Testament in Cologne, expressed his intense opposition to and utter disdain for the whole notion of scripture being translated into the vernacular:

> The New Testament translated into the vulgar tongue is in truth the food of death, the fuel of sin, the veil of malice, the pretext of false liberty, the protection of disobedience, the corruption of discipline, the depravity of morals, the termination of Concord, the death of honesty, the well-spring of vices, the disease of virtues, the instigation of

> rebellion, the milk of pride, the nourishment of contempt, the death of peace, the destruction of charity, the enemy of unity, the murderer of truth.[17]

Here was a man who knew how to hurl an insult!

King Henry condemned Tyndale's New Testament and ordered copies to be burned publically. He also began a policy of persecuting those found guilty of distributing or possessing copies. For his part, Bishop Tunstall authorized a certain merchant who was trading in Antwerp to act as a secret agent of the Crown and use royal funds to buy up every copy he could of the new scripture and send them back to London for burning. What Tunstall didn't know is that the merchant was a sincere friend of Tyndale and thus happily began paying four times the amount it had cost to produce each Tyndale New Testament. "So, for every Bible Tunstall burned, the king paid for three more to be added to Tyndale's arsenal."[18]

A price was now put on Master William's head. Agents of the Crown, bounty hunters really, traveled all over the Continent, sometimes in clever disguise, to track down their criminal. Some of them were bumbling and inept but still treacherous. They could be found bumping into one another but never quite managed to bump into Tyndale; he was spared. Tyndale next went to Marburg, Germany (1527–31) and began working on the Old Testament—translating each word from the original Hebrew text. The Pentateuch (the first five books of Moses) appeared in print in 1530. Tyndale included comments in the margins of his Pentateuch. They were thoroughly Protestant and some anti-papal in tone. At Exodus 36:5–7, for example, where Moses tells the Israelites they do not need to bring any more offerings for the sanctuary, Tyndale wrote, "When will the people say, 'Stop!' and forbid an offering for the building of St. Peter's Church?" Some might remember that it was the construction costs of this project that spurred on the sale of indulgences.[19]

In 1531, Tyndale moved to Antwerp. Controversies over his New Testament translation and subsequent revisions of it, as well as worries over being caught by authorities before his work was completed, distracted him from finishing the translation of the whole Old Testament. However, he was able to add Joshua through 2 Chronicles to the tally of completed books.[20] The rest of the Old Testament would be finished by John Rogers—friend, colleague, and confidante of Master William. But Tyndale never lived to see the whole of his work printed.

Betrayal

Tyndale was a fugitive, and he knew it. One writer commented that he "must have known how a fox feels when the countryside is surrounded by hounds in the hunt."[21] This kind of pressure and its attendant difficulties are known by a select few men and women. Unjust treatment in the face of attempting to follow God's promptings, to do good, and to bless others is often the worst kind of contradiction. Such trials can define or destroy us. But Tyndale did not flinch, did not become embittered or retreat from his own stated conviction that "Scripture derives its authority from him who sent it."[22] John Foxe further reported that Tyndale said, "I call God to record that I have never altered, against the voice of my conscience, one syllable of his Word. Nor would do this day, if all the pleasures, honours, and riches of the earth might be given me."[23]

It was in Antwerp that Tyndale was betrayed and caught by authorities. While living there, he took up residence at the English House, a kind of temporary dormitory to English merchants staying in town. Perhaps because the merchants had protected him so well, Master William let down his guard, which ultimately proved to be a deadly mistake. A secret agent of the English crown, Henry Phillips, claimed to favor the Protestant movement. Tyndale befriended him and even lent him money. In May 1535, Phillips offered to take Tyndale to dinner and lured him into taking a walk through town. As they entered an alley, two captors grabbed Tyndale upon receiving a prearranged signal and quietly whisked him off to the cold, damp dungeon of the Vilvorde fortress near Brussels. There he was imprisoned for almost a year and a half. Though friends and supporters petitioned authorities for his release (they even applied to King Henry), Tyndale was given no reprieve. One of these petitioners, Thomas Poyntz, was himself arrested—guilty by association.[24]

Conditions at Vilvorde dungeon were miserable, as the one surviving letter from the period of Tyndale's incarceration attests.

> I beg your Lordship and that by the Lord Jesus, that if I am to remain here through the winter, you will request the commissary to have the kindness to send me from the goods of mine which he has, a warmer cap: for I suffer greatly from cold in the head, and am afflicted by a perpetual catarrh [a cold] which is much increased in this cell. . . . But most of all I beg you clemency to be urgent with the commissary that he will kindly permit me to have the Hebrew Bible, Hebrew grammar, and Hebrew dictionary that I may pass the time in study. . . . I will be patient abiding the will of God, to the glory of the grace of my Lord Jesus Christ, whose spirit (pray) may ever direct your heart. Amen.[25]

It has been noted that this correspondence sounds very much like one of Paul's letters to Timothy[26] as the former awaited his fate and requested a visit from the latter, saying "the cloke that I left at Troas with Carpus, when thou comest bring with thee, and the books, but especially the parchments" (2 Timothy 4:13). Tyndale's letter hints that he was probably still working on his unfinished translation of the Old Testament.

In August 1536, Master William Tyndale was found guilty of heresy by an ecclesiastical court and delivered over to secular officials for public execution. Again, the principle invoked by the Church, as with the case involving Wycliffe's exhumed body, was *Ecclesia non novit sanguinem*—"the Church does not shed blood."[27] Two months later, on October 6, 1536, Tyndale was taken from his cell, paraded into town, chained to a stake, strangled openly by an executioner with a rope, and then burned. His last coherent words were, "Lord, open the King of England's eyes."[28] One of the great minds and spiritual giants of an already impressive age was dead—his life given for the cause that he believed was God-inspired and that would result in a Bible, in a Restoration, and a changed language that affected the whole world.

Effects of Tyndale's Work

Within a year of Tyndale's death, his dying wish was granted. Tyndale Bibles, or versions that drew heavily upon his work, were circulating in England—now with King Henry's approval. Within two years of Tyndale's death, all parishes were encouraged to have a copy, and within five years, they were ordered to do so or face a fine levied by the government. The mood in the English realm was moving away from support of the papacy. King Henry had been unable to get approval for his divorce from Katherine of Aragon, so Henry was no longer a supporter of the Pope.

Tyndale's influence in other ways is hard to overstate. His translation changed the English language. He replaced certain terms with others that became widely accepted:

"church" (Greek *ecclesia*) became "congregation." "Priest" (Greek *presbyter*) became "elder." "Do penance" (Greek *metanoia*) became "repent." Charity (Greek *agape*) became "love."[29] More than that, literally dozens of words and phrases were invented or coined by Tyndale to make his translation more rich and understandable. That is to say, the words "have no earlier recorded history in written or printed English."[30] These include (but are not limited to):

- alpha and omega
- apple of his eye
- beautiful
- brother's keeper
- busybody
- cast the first stone
- coat of many colors
- eat, drink, and be merry
- infidel
- Jehovah
- judge not
- no man can serve two masters
- Passover
- stiff-necked
- suffer fools gladly
- two-edged sword
- undergird
- ungodly
- uproar

In fact, even the very word at the center of Latter-day Saint theology, "atonement" (at-one-ment) was coined by William Tyndale to describe the reconciliation that occurs between man and God through the redemptive suffering of Jesus Christ. Only someone who understood the infinite and eternal power of Christ's sacrifice to restore humankind back into a right relationship with God the Father after the wrenching estrangement brought about by sin, could have coined the word "atonement." Only someone whose very soul was attuned to the nature of God, to the effects of sin, suffering, repentance, and reconciliation could have coined "atonement." William Tyndale was such a man.

Those of us who share the English-language culture say what we say and are who we are because of William Tyndale. Many of the idioms mentioned above are especially recognized by Latter-day Saints because they are found in Restoration scripture. We are the spiritual heirs of William Tyndale. We are the living beneficiaries of his intellect and spiritual compass.

In addition to the intense effort expended in translation, Master William also wrote other books and tracts that carried tremendous influence. In 1528, he produced two works that became well-known and conveyed powerful messages during the Reformation: *The Parable of the Wicked Mammon* and *The Obedience of a Christian Man*. Consider only one example of their influence: a martyr named Tewkesbury was condemned to the rack at the dread Tower of London because he refused to renounce the Reformation-oriented teachings in *The Parable of the Wicked Mammon*. The reason he gave was that this book had introduced him to Jesus Christ, the Lord, and he wouldn't deny it![31]

Ever the brilliant analyst, William Tyndale saw clearly that one of the major implications of Reformation teaching was what we might call a democratization of God's love—an equalizing or leveling of everyone's standing in the eyes of Deity. This was likely a direct outgrowth of the doctrine of the priesthood of all believers and a disdain for any hint of superiority on the part of clergy and especially the papal court. Tyndale possessed a "low view of the clerical office."[32] He was convinced that lay persons needed no intermediary between themselves and God or between themselves and scripture. But more than that, "Thou that ministereth in the kitchen and are but a kitchen page . . . knoweth that God put thee in that office. . . . [I]f thou compare deed and deed, there is a difference between the washing of dishes and the preaching the word of God; but as touching to please God, none at all."[33] No matter who you are or what you do, you please God if you perform your honest labors with Him in mind. Such was the mindset of William Tyndale.

Conclusion

All that William Tyndale endured, he did for the sake of bringing the word of God to an English-speaking population. Ultimately, he gave everything he possessed—even his own life—for his Lord's work and word. He was a spiritual giant. His work profoundly, even monumentally, influenced future versions of the English Bible. They, in turn, all contributed to the crowning achievement in the chain of English Bibles—the King James Version. But none of these versions equaled the significance of the work accomplished by William Tyndale. "Previous estimates of William Tyndale's contribution to the 1611 King James Version (or Authorized Version) of the Bible have run from a high of up to 90 percent . . . to a low of 18 percent." However, the most recent analysis by researchers at Brigham Young University concludes that for the New Testament, Tyndale's contribution is about 84 percent of the text, while in the Old Testament, about 76 percent of his words have been retained.[34] Tyndale's influence continues to this day.

Notes

1. David Daniell, "William Tyndale, The English Bible, and the English Language," in *The Bible as Book, The Reformation* (London: The British Library & Oak Knoll Press, 2000), 39.
2. Ibid.
3. Ibid, 41.
4. John Foxe, *Foxe's Book of Martyrs*, 135.
5. Ibid, 136.
6. David Daniell, "Introduction," in *The New Testament, A Facsimile of the 1526 Edition*.

7. Foxe, *Foxe's Book of Martyrs*, 136.
8. Ibid, 136, 138.
9. David Daniell, "Introduction."
10. Harold L. Phillips, *Translators and Translations* (Anderson, Indiana: The Warner Press, 1958), 22; English modernized.
11. Quoted in Robert J. Matthews, "A Bible! A Bible!" *Ensign*, Jan. 1987, 22.
12. Connolly, The Indestructible Book, 141.
13. John Foxe, Book of Martyrs, 140.
14. Ibid.
15. Details may be found in almost any history of the period. See John Stevens Kerr, *Ancient Texts Alive Today* (New York: ABS, 1999), 52–53.
16. John Stevens Kerr, *Ancient Texts Alive Today*, 53.
17. Quoted in John Stevens Kerr, *Ancient Texts Alive Today*, 54.
18. W. Kenneth Connolly, *The Indestructible Book*, 142.
19. Miller and Huber, *The Bible: A History*, 170.
20. Kerr, *Ancient Texts Alive Today*, 56.
21. Connolly, *The Indestructible Book*, 142.
22. Ibid, 144.
23. Ibid.
24. Kerr, *Ancient Texts Alive Today*, 60.
25. Ibid.
26. Miller and Huber, *The Bible: A History*, 171.
27. Brian Moynahan, *God's Bestseller*, xi.
28. Kerr, *Ancient Texts Alive Today*, 61.
29. Ibid, 55.
30. Stanly Malless and Jeffrey McQuain, *Coined by God: Words and Phrases that Appear in the English Translations of the Bible* (New York: W. W. Norton & Company, 2003), xiv.
31. Connolly, *The Indestructible Book*, 144.

32. Kerr, *Ancient Texts Alive Today*, 51.
33. Ibid.
34. Jon Nielsen and Royal Skousen, "How Much of the King James Bible is William Tyndale's?" *Reformation* 3 (1998), 74.

7.

A Bible Fit *for* Monarchs *and* Prophets

The King James Version

William Tyndale's martyrdom must have caused the heavens to weep, but it also caused his associates to steel their resolve and redouble their efforts. Master William became only one of several others who learned by personal experience that the Adversary hates and spurns the scriptures, that he will do anything to keep the world from having more scripture circulate, and that he delights in making war on saintly souls—people like William Tyndale.

John Rogers was another such man. Rogers was Tyndale's friend and was responsible for completing the translation of the Old Testament into English, getting it to press, and ultimately becoming a martyr for the cause of truth.

John Rogers' brief friendship with Tyndale began in Antwerp and had a profound effect on Rogers. He believed Tyndale's work and vision to be so important that he guarded with his life all the unpublished Old Testament translations and handwritten notes Tyndale had left with him for safe keeping. He had the completed Bible published under the pseudonym of Thomas Matthew in 1537, just one year after Tyndale's death. At the insistence of Archbishop Thomas Cranmer, the "Matthews Bible" was granted the "Kings most gracious license" and officially recognized in England. Tyndale's heavenward plea to open the English king's eyes, which Tyndale uttered at the time of his execution, was now answered!

Eventually Rogers forsook the priesthood and the Roman Catholic Church, married a woman from Antwerp, and became pastor of a Protestant congregation in Wittenberg, Germany (hometown of Luther and, for a brief time, Tyndale himself). He then returned to England during the reign of King Edward VI (1547–1553), who was sympathetic to Reform. In time, Rogers was recognized for his abilities at preaching and pastoring and was appointed lecturer in divinity at St. Paul's in London.[1]

When Queen Mary I (1553–1558), a Catholic, ascended the English throne upon the death of Edward VI, the Reform-friendly atmosphere evaporated, and many Reformation leaders fled the continent. John Rogers, however, was defiant. In July 1553, he preached a sermon at St. Paul's on "the true doctrine taught in King Edward's days," and warned everyone to beware of returning to "pestilent Popery."[2] Ten days later, he was put under house arrest. In January 1554, he was sent to Newgate Prison in London for a year and then dispatched to the residence of a notorious persecutor of Reformers for an interview. Finally, in late January 1555, Rogers was convicted, by a papal commission, of denying the Christian character of the Roman Catholic Church and rejecting the doctrine of transubstantiation by saying that the bread and wine of the Lord's Supper did not turn into the actual body and blood of Christ. For Rogers, such a denial was in perfect harmony with scriptural warrant. Transubstantiation was not a biblical doctrine. But biblical or not, Rogers was sentenced to death.

On February 4, 1555, John Rogers was taken to

Smithfield, where he was burned at the stake, becoming the first Christian Martyr of Queen Mary's reign.[3] It is said that Rogers awaited and met death cheerfully. He was accompanied to his execution by his wife and, by then, eleven children. The French ambassador to England witnessed the spectacle and was moved to observe that Rogers was given such support by the greatest part of the people and was so comforted by his children that "it seemed more like he was [being] led to a wedding than to his death."[4] Rogers' fellow prisoner, John Bradford, said Rogers "broke the ice valiantly."[5] Here were men and women who looked to a home beyond the grave, who fully expected that a better life awaited them in the company of the Lord. They were very much in the mold of the Apostle Paul, whose words they read thoroughly: "For to me to live is Christ, and to die is gain" (Philippians 1:21).

Queen Mary I, the daughter of King Henry VIII and his first wife, Katharine of Aragon, is described as being filled with resentment over the way Henry treated her mother.[6] Henry had unsuccessfully attempted to have their twenty-four-year marriage annulled because Katharine couldn't provide a surviving male heir to the English throne, and Henry didn't want Mary to become monarch. The resultant divorce and departure from the Catholic Church set in motion events that resulted in the English Reformation. However, this departure was also a major factor contributing to the intensity of the Catholic restoration Mary pursued and the bloodbath over which she presided.

Many Protestants were executed during the period known as the Marian Persecutions—a time when the queen ordered the wholesale executions of Reformers and anti-Catholic agitators unfortunate enough to come within her orbit. The first round of executions began with John Rogers and lasted five days. During this time, three other men were put to death: Lawrence Saunders on February 8 and

Rowland Taylor and John Hooper, Bishop of Gloucester, on February 9. The extended period of persecution lasted for almost four years. When the fires of death finally died down, 284 individuals had been executed, most by burning.[7] This tragic period of persecution earned for the queen the title, "Bloody Mary."

Thomas Bilney (1495–1531), another contemporary of William Tyndale, suffered martyrdom as a direct result of the new era of biblical translation, but before Queen Mary ascended the throne. Bilney was born in Norwich, England, educated at Cambridge University, and was ordained a priest (took holy orders) by 1519. But he felt that his "religious life was barren." Finding no peace or satisfaction in his labors, he began studying Erasmus' edition of the Greek New Testament, published three years earlier, and had a life-changing experience. He recorded that when he came across the words of St. Paul in 1 Timothy 1:15, he "felt a marvellous comfort and quietness, insomuch that my bruised bones lept for joy."[8] The words of Paul that changed him? "This is a faithful saying, and worthy of all acceptation, that Christ Jesus came into the world to save sinners; of whom I am the chief."

Bilney's experience, including the impact of Paul's written testimony, which was very much central to it, sounds a lot like Martin Luther's life-changing experience, which also resulted from reading a declaration of Paul's—in his epistle to the Romans (see Romans 1:14; 2–3). The scriptures were central to Bilney's life. As he studied the word of God, doubt gave way to faith, turmoil was replaced by peace, and he was filled with a desire to share his new life in Christ with others. The White Horse Inn became the meeting place of Cambridge scholars who congregated to discuss Bilney's ideas, which sprang forth from the New Testament.[9] He greatly influenced and even inspired others at Cambridge in doctrine and in charitable works.[10] One of these was Hugh Latimer, an English theologian who was also later burned at the stake on Broad Street in Oxford because of his "reforming" views.[11]

In 1525, Bilney became licensed to preach from the pulpit by the bishop of Ely. He denounced practices not in harmony with scripture, particularly the worship of saints and relics.[12] He was arrested while preaching in Ipswich, taken to the dreaded Tower of London, and tried in Westminster. His judges included Cardinal Wolsey, the Archbishop of Canterbury, and several other bishops and lawyers. Through conversations with his friends (similar to those that Job had in ancient times), Bilney's resolve to withstand intense opposition was undermined, and he was persuaded to recant his theological positions on the grounds that to do so would really be the best for Reformation efforts.

The Sunday following his recantation (December 7, 1527) Bilney walked to St. Paul's Cathedral with a shaven head, was made to listen to a sermon denouncing his own heretical ideas, and forced to set fire to a stack of Tyndale Bibles. It is said that for a time his soul was shattered and his mind nearly deranged. But ultimately he resolved to get re-arrested in order to stand up for doctrines he believed to be true. Since churches were no longer open to him, he preached in open-air venues—fields and village squares—to any and all who would listen. He finally got his wish and was arrested again, this time in Norwich.[13]

Bilney's second trial occurred in 1531. He was degraded from his orders (unfrocked), sentenced to execution, and handed over to civil magistrates to be burned to death. The night before his death, he was eating his last meal when friends came to visit him in order to comfort him in the face of the horrible ordeal that awaited the following day. In an attempt to display his eagerness to suffer for the Lord's sake, he stuck his finger in the flame of a candle and pointed to a passage in Isaiah 43:2: "When thou walkest through fire, thou shalt not be burned."[14] Of course his finger was burned—badly—but his spirits were never better.

On the morning of August 19, 1531, Bilney was led from his cell by his captors to the place of execution—Lollards Pit in Norwich. As the group was crossing Bishop's bridge, Bilney ran forward to the stake which awaited him, embraced it, and thanked God for the chance to make things right and die for Christ.

Though Thomas Bilney was not actively involved in translating the Bible into English or other vernacular tongues, he has been regarded as the "man who may perhaps be called the initiator" in the new cycle of translations of the Bible into English beginning with Tyndale.[15] He helped establish the theological environment that called for such a translation, and which then allowed it to thrive. He also lived a life that served as "a noble example to his contemporaries. First, he taught the reformers how to live for Christ, and then he taught them how to die for Him."[16]

Bishop's Bridge in Norwich, England, which Thomas Bilney crossed on the way to his execution (AD 1531).

Responses

Queen Elizabeth (1558–1603) followed Queen Mary on the throne of the English realm. Protestants everywhere breathed a sigh of relief. Many people had gone to prison or had been put to death across Europe over the years for supporting reform of the Roman Church, which included the spread of Bibles in the vernacular. But European religious reform in general, and the English Reformation in particular, was by then unstoppable. Throughout the British Isles, the Bible in English had become the heart and core of earth-shaking change, as historian G. M. Trevelyan noted: "The English Reformation, which had begun as a Parliamentary attack on Church fees, and proceeded as a royal raid on Abbey lands, was at last to find its religious basis in the popular knowledge of the Scriptures which had been the dream of Wycliffe."[17]

By the time King James (1603-1625) succeeded Queen Elizabeth to the throne of England, reactions to the translation of the Bible into English were many and varied, exemplified in the several versions of the Bible in English that had appeared since Tyndale's New Testament was first published in 1526. The main versions were the Coverdale Bible of 1535 (named after its editor); the Great Bible of 1539 (named for its size); the Geneva Bible of 1560 (named for its place of printing); the Bishop's Bible of 1568 (authorized by the Church of England clergy); and the Catholic Douai-Rheims Bible of 1582 (so named for the place of translation—Douai Rheims College).

But each of these Bibles favored a different religious viewpoint. The Geneva Bible contained a running commentary that was intensely antagonistic toward the Pope and the Roman Catholic hierarchy, the Church of England, and the universities. However, the Geneva Bible was immensely popular with the people. It is undoubtedly the version Shakespeare used. It is the Bible that came to America on the Mayflower, and it was certainly the version read by our Pilgrim forefathers. Yet it was understandably annoying to the bishops of the Church of England, and because it was so bluntly biased, it actually left Puritans nervous. Not least, it made the new King unhappy. It was too Protestant![18] The English clergy's response to the Geneva Bible was the Bishop's Bible, proposed by Matthew Parker, Archbishop of Canterbury, and translated by a goodly number of Church bishops.

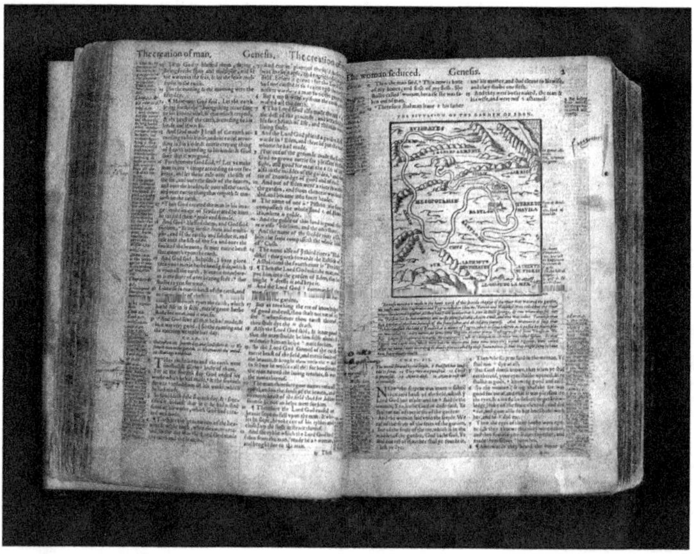

Pages of the Geneva Bible (AD 1560). Notice the marginal notes.

Parker was a good man and fine scholar. He sacrificed much for the truth as he understood it. He rose to become vice-chancellor of Cambridge University. But during her reign, Queen Mary stripped Parker of his offices, and he lived in obscurity until Queen Elizabeth elevated him to the Archbishopric. Whereas the Geneva Bible was filled with anti-Catholic annotations, Parker ordered that the Bishop's Bible avoid notes of a doctrinal or controversial nature.[19]

Still, the Puritans were not happy with it because, as they said, it was not accurate, which was true for some portions.

The Puritans argued that the Church and society needed to be "purified" of all remnants of Catholic influence. This meant anything that resembled the Roman Church or distorted Christianity from their point of view, which included such items as the office of bishop, clerical robes, emphasis on "high Church" rituals, and the popular versions of the Bible currently in use. Therefore, before King James even got to London to take up his new duties, he was presented with the Millenary Petition, so called because it was signed by 1,000 Puritans who requested changes in the Church of England, including a new Bible.

James VI of Scotland had ruled over the Scottish realm for many years before he became King of England in 1603. He liked the Episcopal (bishop-centered) structure of the Church of England. He especially liked the Church's title for the king, "Defender of the Faith." He was not anxious to change things. Yet on one matter he agreed with the Puritans—the kingdom needed a new translation of the Bible.

In January 1604, during his first regnal year in England, James called a conference at Hampton Court Palace to evaluate the condition of the Church of England. The conference did not favor Puritans. The King told them to accept the Church as it was or he would "harry [force] them out of the land."[20] But he did agree to proceed with plans for a new Bible, with the provision that it omit controversial notes like those in the Geneva Bible.[21]

Work on the new Bible began in July. The king claimed to have appointed fifty-four men to the translation team, although only fifty names can be found on various surviving lists. These men were divided into six translation companies, two companies each working from three different cities in England (Oxford, Cambridge, and Westminster in London), and included the finest biblical scholars of that era. Dr. Lancelot Andrewes, for example, was a brilliant linguist, master of fifteen languages, Dean of Westminster, and a famous preacher and devotional writer. William Bedwell of Cambridge University was the father of Arabic studies in England and the most distinguished Islamicist of his day. Dr. Miles Smith was a fine Semiticist, an energetic Puritan, and scribe of the King James Bible Preface. Sir Henry Savile was eminent among Greek scholars and the one to whom his wife once said, "I wish I were a book. Then you would respect me."[22] Surely, these were men prepared for the very purpose to which they applied their considerable abilities.

These men sought not their own aggrandizement but the

Hampton Court Palace outside London, where the conference was convened to make plans for the King James Version.

will of God. It was Miles Smith who said they didn't start out to make a new translation of the Bible because others were bad. Rather, they desired "to make a good one better, or out of many good ones, one principal good one . . . that hath been our endeavour, that our mark. To that purpose there were many [scholars] chosen, that were greater in other men's eyes then [sic] in their own, and that sought the truth rather than their own praise."[23]

It is no exaggeration to say these translators worked long and hard to produce a new version of the word of God. In fact, some of them turned every waking moment to the task. One example is John Bois. Born in 1560, by age six, Bois could read Hebrew and write the Hebrew alphabet with elegance. As an undergraduate at Cambridge University, he studied from 4:00 AM to 8:00 PM and turned down a career in medicine to pursue theology and humanities. He was assigned to the sixth company of translators working on the Apocrypha. He worked all week at St. John's College, only to return to his country parish on weekends to prepare and deliver his Sunday sermons. Some objected to the appointment of this "country preacher" to a translation team filled with the ranks of such notable scholars from all over England. However, John Bois loved God and the common man. His work ethic was such that he did not waste a spare moment. And he believed in the importance of the work, though he did not believe himself to be important. Dr. Bois was ultimately chosen to do the final editing work on the entire biblical manuscript and prepare it for the press.[24]

One scholar who was not chosen for the original translation team became a vicious opponent of the new Bible, even though he had first argued for it. Hugh Broughton, a renowned professor, apparently became so incensed at not receiving an invitation to participate that he would later write in a letter, "Tell His Majesty, I had rather be rent in pieces with wild horses, than any such translation by my consent should be urged upon poor churches. . . . The new edition crosseth me. I require it to be burnt."[25] Though Broughton was admittedly a very bright man, he was also

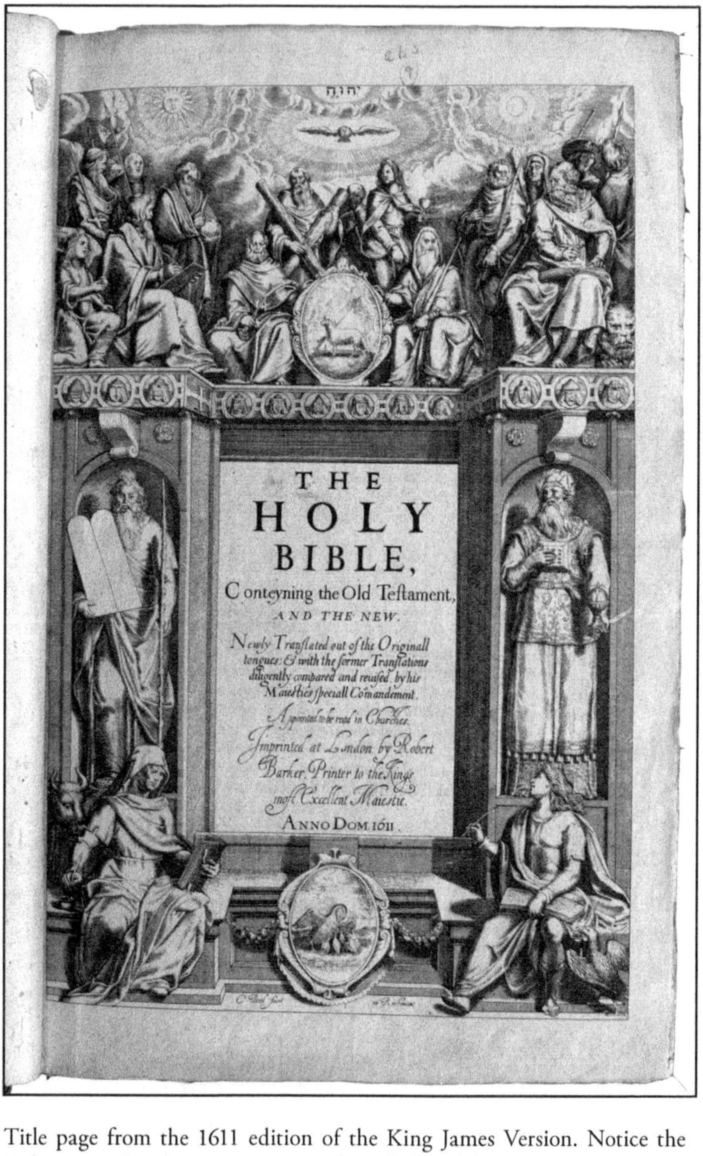

Title page from the 1611 edition of the King James Version. Notice the Hebrew word at the top center, signifying "Jehovah"

a cantankerous old egotist. He was not missed, owing to his eccentricity and bad temper, nor did his absence from the translation team impoverish the work. In spite of his opposition, the results of some work he did on a planned independent translation of the Bible found its way into the hands of the King James translation team anyway.[26]

The King James Bible has also been called the "Authorized Version," though, oddly enough, no proof has survived that the king formally approved the final product. Officially, the new version was "appointed to be read in churches," to replace the Bishop's Bible.[27] But it was a long time before the King James Version displaced the Geneva Bible as the Bible read by individuals. Once established, however, the King James Version became entrenched. It took more than two hundred fifty years before a serious attempt was made to replace the King James Version with an updated translation. The English Revised Version appeared in 1885. From this revision sprang an American variation called the American Standard Version in 1901. This was followed by the Revised Standard Version in 1952 and the New Revised Standard Version in 1989.[28] In 1978, the New International Version appeared, with revisions in subsequent years.

Many of these versions undertook to correct mistakes found in the King James Bible. Early editions of the King James Bible were plagued with misprints, which were corrected in later printings. But one example of a misprint that never got corrected is found in Matthew 23:24, "strain at a gnat." It originally read "strain out a gnat." It has been corrected in other versions of the Bible.

Because of these so-called problems and the archaic nature of seventeenth-century English, some people say the King James Version is too outdated and will soon become obsolete (or should become obsolete). Latter-day Saints disagree. It is not obsolete! Even if the King James Version were to someday go out of print—which is unlikely[29]—the English language still bulges with such immortal expressions as

- The skin of my teeth (Job 19:20)
- Woe is me! (Psalm 120:5)
- A drop in a bucket (Isaiah 40:15)
- My brother's keeper (Genesis 4:9)
- Holier than thou (Isaiah 65:5)
- At their wits' end (Psalm 107:27)
- Hair stood on end (Job 4:15)
- Apple of his eye (Psalm 17:8)
- Lily of the valley (Song of Solomon 2:1)
- Line upon line (Isaiah 28:10)
- Set house in order (Isaiah 38:1)
- Can a leopard change its spots? (Jeremiah 13:23)
- Hollow of his hand (Isaiah 40:12)

More than that, the Restoration of the gospel is tied to the King James Version. In a First Presidency letter dated May 22, 1992, and addressed to all priesthood leaders in English-speaking units, the following counsel was given by Presidents Benson, Hinckley, and Monson:

> Many versions of the Bible are available today. Unfortunately, no original manuscripts of any portion of the Bible are available for comparison to determine the most accurate version. However, the Lord has revealed clearly the doctrines of the gospel in these latter days. The most reliable way to measure the accuracy of any biblical passage is not by comparing different texts, but by comparison with the Book of Mormon and modern-day revelations.
>
> While other Bible versions may be easier to read than the King James Version, in doctrinal

> matters latter-day revelation supports the King James Version in preference to other English translations. All of the Presidents of the Church, beginning with the Prophet Joseph Smith, have supported the King James Version by encouraging its continued use in the Church. In light of all the above, it is the English language Bible used by The Church of Jesus Christ of Latter-day Saints.[30]

Today, most people who can quote from the Bible quote the King James Version published in 1611. As one source notes, modern-day translators of new Bible revisions may "rightly feel humble," knowing they can never produce a work that will so mold a language, shape an entire culture, and change the whole world, as did the King James Version.[31]

New translations of the Bible continue to be made for a variety of reasons: to keep apace of changes in the language; to facilitate ease of understanding; and occasionally to harmonize language with theological understandings in the modern world. (It must be recognized that any translation is automatically an interpretation.) However, nothing yet has quite hit the highwater mark left by the King James Version.

The King James Version of the Bible was the culmination of a long process and many participants. We owe a great debt to all those who made the English Bible possible. Their sacrifices were monumental and their faith inspiring.

Notes

1. Connolly, *The Indestructible Book*, 150.
2. Ibid.
3. Ibid, 151.
4. Kerr, *Ancient Texts Alive Today*, 70.
5. Connolly, *The Indestructible Book*, 151.

6. Kerr, *Ancient Texts Alive Today*, 86.
7. Eamon Duffy, *Fires of Faith: Catholic England Under Mary Tudor* (New Haven: Yale, 2008), 79.
8. http://en.wikipedia.org/wiki/Thomas_Bilney. See also James Simpson, *Burning to Read* (Cambridge: Harvard University Press, 2007), 57.
9. Elisabeth Leedham-Green, *A Concise History of the University of Cambridge* (Cambridge: Cambridge University Press, 2001), 44.
10. Ibid, 45.
11. Simpson, *Burning to Read*, 41–42.
12. Connolly, *The Indestructible Book*, 126–27.
13. Ibid, 127–128
14. Ibid, 128.
15. Ibid, 125.
16. Ibid, 128.
17. George M. Trevelyan, *History of England*, (London: Loungman) II:65.
18. Miller and Huber, *The Bible: A History*, 178.
19. Kerr, *Ancient Texts Alive Today*, 97–98.
20. Miller and Huber, *The Bible: A History*, 178.
21. Kerr, *Ancient Texts Alive Today*, 113.
22. Ibid, 115.
23. Ibid, 117.
24. Ibid, 121.
25. Miller and Huber, *The Bible: A History*, 180.
26. Kerr, *Ancient Texts Alive Today*, 115, 129.
27. "Publication of the King James Bible," *Christian History*, Issue 28 (vol. IX, no. 4), 43–44.
28. See the chart in John Stevens Kerr, *Ancient Texts Alive Today*, 203–207.
29. "Publication of the King James Bible," *Christian History*, 44.
30. Reprinted in the *Ensign*, August 1992, 80.

31. "Publication of the King James Bible," *Christian History*, 44.

8.

The Place of the English Bible in the Restoration

The great work of the Restoration of the gospel of Jesus Christ in these last days has been foreknown by God from the beginning (Abraham 2:8). Many souls have contributed to its fulfillment. Elder Robert D. Hales has stated, "Through the inspired sacrifices of God's children through the ages, the foundation of the Restoration was laid, and the world is preparing for the Second Coming of our Lord and Savior Jesus Christ. . . . Making the scriptures available and helping God's children learn to read them was the first step to the Restoration of the gospel."[1]

It is both right and proper to memorialize the efforts of all those Reformers and translators who served as forerunners to the Restoration and helped create a widely acceptable and reliable edition of the biblical text in English. Nothing has had greater influence in laying the foundation for the Restoration of the Gospel of Jesus Christ in this final dispensation than the English Bible, culminating with the King James Version. Consider the following:

- The English Bible preceded the Book of Mormon in the timetable of the Restoration.
- The English Bible was instrumental in changing the religious and political climate of Europe and in

bringing about the great religious revolution called the Reformation, the seedbed of the Restoration.

- The English Bible was central to the establishment of America, again a prerequisite for the Restoration.
- The now-famous passage in the book of James (chapter 1, verse 5) in the King James Version led directly to the First Vision.
- The Book of Mormon was translated into English using the vernacular of the King James Version.
- The language of the other standard works borrows from the linguistic structure and idiom of the English Bible.
- From the very earliest days of the Restoration, members of The Church of Jesus Christ of Latter-day Saints were commanded to teach the principles of the gospel "which are in the Bible" (D&C 42:12)—which, at that time, was the King James Bible.
- The revision of the Bible now known as the Joseph Smith Translation was based on the King James Version.
- The King James Bible has received the strong endorsement of LDS Church leaders to the present day.

Three foundational and interrelated preparations were put in place so that the Restoration of the gospel in the latter days could proceed. These are the same three preparations put in place back in the meridian dispensation so that the gospel of Jesus Christ could be restored and established by Jesus and the Apostles in the Roman world.

1. A widely accepted translation of the Bible in the dominant language and tied to the dominant culture of the period.
2. A stable political system to provide a base of

operation from which the Restoration could go forward.

3. A culture and language which fostered the establishment of the gospel, including a spirit of restoration which anticipated a new dispensation.

In the meridian dispensation, the Bible that served as the basis for the restoration of the first century (Christ's meridian Church was a restoration) was the Septuagint—the Greek translation of the Old Testament from the original Hebrew. It had been in place for more than two hundred years, was common to all, and was tied to the pervasive Greek culture of the period. In the nineteenth century, the Bible undergirding the Restoration was the King James Version—the latest iteration of English Bibles made from previous English translations and the available Hebrew and Greek texts of the Old and New Testaments. It had been in place for two hundred years.

In the meridian dispensation, the governmental system that allowed for the gospel to be established in a stable political environment (for its day) was the Roman Empire. It was largely the creation of one man, Octavian, called Caesar Augustus (31 BC–AD 14), who established it on the foundations of the Roman Republic. It was so well founded and provided such a period of peace and prosperity that the Roman Empire survived its founder for several hundred years (even with subsequent incompetent and wicked emperors at its helm) and left a legacy known as the Pax Romana (Roman Peace).

In preparation for the latter-day Restoration in the nineteenth century, the United States of America had been recently established. The system of government prepared by the Lord was grounded in the Constitution of the United States (D&C 101:77–80), including the Bill of Rights and the principles articulated in the Declaration of Independence.

In the meridian dispensation, the language and culture of the Mediterranean world that allowed for the restored Gospel of Jesus Christ to take root and flourish for a season was Greek. In the nineteenth century, the English language and culture provided the seedbed for the flowering of the Restored gospel. Both eras were filled with an expectation of restoration. Both eras witnessed its fulfillment after the right elements had been put in place—culture and language, stable political system, and a widely accepted translation of the Bible.

Thus, the English Bible is at the heart of who we are as Latter-day Saints. It is the scriptural heritage bequeathed to us by faith-filled translators; it is a reflection of their discipleship. The English Bible is a testimony to their conviction that all of God's children deserved the opportunity to personally read (or hear) God's communications to them from the pages of the sacred canon without having to get them through the filter of a human intermediary such as a priest or bishop. These remarkable, self-sacrificing witnesses and evangelists believed biblical doctrines deserved to be carried to the heart of every Christian disciple firsthand and not be left only to the purview of Churchmen or scholars who knew Latin, Greek, or Hebrew. This modest book is a testament to the faith of those who gave us the Bible in English, who truly believed that God was no respecter of persons and that he cares for all his children and desires for them the opportunity to have access to all truth, uncorrupted and unembellished.

Today we live in peace, but it wasn't always so. Today we enjoy a relatively calm religious environment, but it wasn't always so. Today we have access to whatever version of the Bible suits us, but it wasn't always so. Today we are flooded with light, but it wasn't always so. We sometimes forget that the peace, calm, light, and availability of our scriptures came at a dear price. But the beliefs for which hundreds of souls gave their lives were not lost. Many millions have come to experience for themselves what William Tyndale, and many like him, taught: "The nature of God's word is, that whosoever read it, . . . it will begin immediately to make him every day better and better, till he be grown into a perfect man."[2]

Though conflict swept across Europe decade after decade over the individual's right to possess and read scripture for himself or herself, gradually "the dark night of ignorance [came] to an end. Declared one preacher before being burned, 'We shall this day light such a candle, by God's Grace . . . as I trust shall never be put out.'"[3]

Indeed, by God's grace the light has not been put out nor will it be. Reformers, translators, and martyrs did their part. We must now do ours. Said Elder Robert D. Hales:

> In the Lord's service the path is not always easy. It often requires sacrifices, and we will likely experience adversity. But in serving Him, we discover that His hand is truly over us. So it was for Wycliffe, Tyndale, and thousands of others who prepared the way for the Restoration. So it was for the Prophet Joseph Smith and all who helped usher in the restored gospel. So it is and will be for us. The Lord expects us to be as faithful, as devoted, as courageous as those who went before us. They were called to give their lives for the gospel. We are called to live our lives for the same purpose.[4]

We can never repay those who gave so much, in many cases their "all," for the cause of bringing forth the English Bible—a Bible fit for the Restoration. But we can read the Bible, honor it, live and proclaim its messages of life and salvation to those we meet. These forerunners of the Restoration whom we have highlighted in previous pages were called to die for the gospel. We are asked to live for it. "If God spare my life" ought to be our covenant words just as they were theirs. May we remember 2011, the four-hundredth anniversary of the King James Version of the Bible, as the time when we reconfirmed our efforts to do all we can to study and then live the words that came at such a dear price.

Notes

1. Robert D. Hales, "Preparations for the Restoration and the Second Coming: 'My Hand Shall Be Over Thee,'" *Ensign*, November 2005, 88.
2. Quoted in Robert Hales, "Preparation for the Restoration," 89.
3. Ibid.
4. Ibid.

Index of Persons

M

N

P

R

S

T

V

W

X

Z

About *the* Author

Andrew C. Skinner is a former dean of Religious Education at Brigham Young University, Provo, Utah (2000–2005). He served as executive director of the Neal A. Maxwell Institute for Religious Scholarship at BYU from 2005–2008. In Fall 2010, he was appointed Richard L. Evans Professor of Religious Understanding. He is Professor of Ancient Scripture and Near Eastern Studies, a member of the international editorial group that worked on the Dead Sea Scrolls, and the author or co-author of over 200 articles and books on religious and historical topics.

Brother Skinner is a graduate of the University of Colorado and holds master's degrees from Iliff School of Theology and Harvard University in Hebrew Bible and Judaic Studies, and a PhD degree in European and Near Eastern history from the University of Denver. He pursued graduate studies at Hebrew University in Jerusalem and has taught at BYU's Jerusalem Center for Near Eastern Studies on four different occasions, most recently from August 2008 through August 2009.

Brother Skinner has served in various callings in the LDS Church, including bishop, a member of the Church's Correlation Evaluation Committee, and a member of the Sunday School General Board. He is married to Janet Corbridge Skinner, and they are the parents of six children. He taught at then Ricks College from 1988 to 1992, and before that at the University of Colorado.

0 26575 59087 6